Federal Aerial Firefighting: Assessing Safety and Effectiveness

Blue Ribbon Panel Report to the Chief, USDA Forest Service and Director, USDI Bureau of Land Management

December 2002

Contents

Executive Summary

In response to the 2002 fire season's fatal aircraft accidents, the USDA Forest Service and USDI Bureau of Land Management (BLM) jointly established an independent, five-member Blue Ribbon Commission (the panel – Appendix A) to identify essential information for planning a safe and effective future aviation program. On August 15, 2002, the Chief of the Forest Service and Director of the BLM asked the panel to identify weaknesses and fail points in the current aviation program, focusing on safety, operational effectiveness, costs, sustainability, and strategic guidance. Assuming an integrated approach, the agencies tasked the panel to address these five areas as they relate to the operation and supervision of air tankers, lead planes and air supervision modules, helicopters, and air attack platforms (Appendix B).

Within a 90-day period, the panel held town hall meetings in Atlanta, Portland, Salt Lake City, Denver, Albuquerque, and Sacramento, soliciting comments and ideas from those with an interest in the federal firefighting aviation program. The Federal Aviation Administration, National Transportation Safety Board, California Department of Forestry and Fire Protection, and Canadian and United States air tanker operators, Conair and Aerounion, respectively, also provided special briefings to the panel. Verbal and written remarks were received from aerial firefighting-industry officials, air tanker contractors, aircraft manufacturers, fixed-wing and helicopter pilots, private-sector consultants, and concerned people. In addition, the panel heard commentary from representatives of state and federal agencies responsible for fighting wildland fires.

The massive amount of material and brief time for analysis forced the panel to address, for the most part, only major considerations. *Possibly the single largest challenge now facing leaders of these federal agencies is to foster cooperation and collaboration among working-level staffs, contractors, and states to raise the standards of aerial wildland firefighting in the United States.* This report presents eight key findings, which the panel believes are critical for planning a safe and effective future firefighting aviation program. The panel relied significantly on the knowledge, experience, and judgment of its members to develop its findings, which are strong inferences rather than deduced certainties. The panel's mandate was to identify problems, not advocate solutions or make recommendations

FINDING 1–SAFETY

The safety record of fixed-wing aircraft and helicopters used in wildland fire management is unacceptable.

The panel determined that contractor personnel flying large air tankers are subject to a lower safety standard than government personnel flying federally owned and operated lead planes and smoke-jumper aircraft. Further, the level of safety for both contractor and government aerial firefighting operations is lower than can be financially justified, and is less than expected for any employer concerned about its employees. This disparity in safety standards stems from a government contracting process that assumes the airworthiness of today's large air tanker fleet has been assured by the FAA's type certification process. However, responsibility for the continued airworthiness of aircraft converted to air tankers is up to the contractors who own and operate the aircrafts.

The panel saw no reports that identified in-flight structural failures or break-ups of helicopters. However, in reviewing a document that summarized 36 aviation accidents related to fire service rotorcraft during the past 10 years, there were many accidents with similar features. The panel also found that varying airworthiness standards required under federal firefighting contracts had an impact on helicopter safety. However, much of the helicopter work associated with firefighting is consistent with the rotorcraft's original mission design.

The Forest Service owns and operates a fleet of 19 pressurized Beechcraft Baron BE-58P aircraft. Although flown in a variety of roles, the Barons' principal mission is to serve as lead planes for large air tankers. Many lead plane missions are flown over mountainous terrain during summer months when temperatures are well above those of a standard day. Under these conditions, air density is much lower than at sea level, which reduces the capability of an aircraft to maintain altitude. In addition, much of the terrain in fire-prone regions, particularly in the western United States, is higher than the Baron's single-engine service ceiling, which is the maximum altitude that a multiengine aircraft can maintain a 50-foot/minute rate of climb when flying on one engine. The Baron fleet is also experiencing a high rate of maintenance problems, raising concerns about the long-term sustainability of safe operations. The structural life expectancy for Barons flying the firefighting mission also is questionable. It would appear that Baron operations cannot be easily limited to missions that can be conducted safely, and there are no other suitable aircraft available to assume firefighting functions.

Damage-resistant voice and data recorders on aircraft are essential for effective accident investigations. However, no Forest Service or BLM policy requires recorders to be installed on either government-owned or contractor-flown aircraft.

FINDING 2—NEW ENVIRONMENT, NEW RISKS

Because the wildland environment has changed significantly, controlling wildland fires cannot be considered an auxiliary mission second to land management. Wildland firefighting has grown to a level of importance that warrants the attention of national leaders.

Much of the nation has been subjected to prolonged and severe drought since 1996, which has created, in some areas, the worst fire danger experienced in more than 100 years. Forest Service data indicate that as of October 2002 nearly 50% of the United States landmass "continues to be in a moderate-to-extreme state of drought." Development of a wildland-urban interface has forced today's managers to contend with entirely different options. People are increasingly moving into rural areas, building homes, ranchettes, summer cabins, condominium complexes, and communities in and adjacent to public lands. Significantly different firefighting philosophies and tactics are required when fires threaten developed areas. Fires consumed 8.4 million acres of United

States wildland in 2000, and 6.8 million acres burned in 2002, which is nearly double the 10-year average. The environmental conditions that created today's threat of large fires have taken decades to develop and are not the fault of any political party or federal land management agency. The conditions evolved from uncoordinated policy changes that responded largely to public demands and have been exacerbated by shifting demographics, severe drought, and a drastic change in the national security landscape.

FINDING 3–AIRCRAFT

Under the current system of aircraft certification, contracting, and operation, key elements of the aerial wildland firefighting fleet are unsustainable.

Recent in-flight structural failures signaled the recurrence of a problem that has periodically plagued firefighting air tankers for half a century. This is the end of a third type of aircraft cycle, which have each culminated in accidents and crew fatalities. Each cycle begins with the Forest Service and its private-sector contractors obtaining retired military bombers, transports, and patrol aircraft from the Pentagon's "boneyard." Stripping-out unneeded systems to reduce weight, contractors outfit the air tankers with fire retardant tanks and delivery systems, obtain FAA Restricted Category type certificates, and put the aircraft into firefighting service. There are a few nonmilitary exceptions, such as FAA-certified commercial air transports converted to air tankers, but, to the panel's knowledge, none of these have suffered catastrophic structural failures.

Private operators, for the most part, have done an admirable job of keeping these aging aircraft flying. However, they are handicapped by receiving little, if any, support from former military operators and the aircraft's original manufacturer. Additionally, the FAA has essentially said, "It's a public-use aircraft. You're on your own." There are few checks and balances to ensure that the aircraft are airworthy and safe to fly throughout a fire season. Contractors have no financial incentive and are not required to ensure that their aircraft are safe to fly. A number of potentially viable options were routinely dismissed as too expensive before being carefully examined, perhaps reflecting this community's "no-money" state-of-mind. The panel was told that both government employees and contractors assume that Congress, the administration, and federal agencies will never provide the money needed to do the firefighting job correctly and safely, leaving them to manage with whatever Forest Service and BLM budgets allow.

The panel, recognizing that a systems-level approach is needed to improve the current large air tanker situation, sought technical information that would quantify the actual stresses large air tankers are subjected to when fighting a fire, particularly in mountainous terrain, however, little data were available. The most telling data came from a 1974 NASA Langley Research Center report, *Operating Experiences of Retardant Bombers During Firefighting* indicating that flight loads and maneuver aggressiveness actually experienced by the DC-6Bs exceeded pilot estimates.

The long-term sustainability of the Baron fleet, particularly from a structural standpoint, must be considered in doubt. The panel heard that, in the absence of a rigorous engineering analysis backed by flight test data and FAA review, it is not possible to ensure that the aircraft are airworthy to continue operating as firefighting lead planes. Because most of the fire suppression and support helicopter fleet is FAA-certified and generally operated within the limits of their design while firefighting, the panel has little reason to question the fleet's near-term sustainability. The only concern voiced during presentations was related to ex-military helicopters, which are operated under a Restricted Category type certificate, and must be considered FAA "orphans," similar to the ex-military air tanker situation.

FINDING 4–MISSION

The variety of missions, philosophies, and unclear standards of federal land management agencies creates a "mission muddle" that seriously compromises the safety and effectiveness of aviation in wildland fire management.

The panel believes that aerial firefighting risks remain higher than necessary because the mission differences among agencies have not been recognized, reconciled, and expressed as a common operations plan with clear lines of authority. The efficiency and safety of air operations could be markedly increased by such a plan, which also could mitigate the perception that resources are not being well used. Jurisdictions and federal- and state-agency responsibilities must be reconciled to develop a more effective national wildland aerial firefighting program. Many mandates are based on constitutional arrangements, and it will likely be difficult to share duties and delegate or transfer activities. But with the right motivation, such reorganizations are possible.

The panel is aware of useful, well-intentioned interagency coordination and cooperation arrangements, and these represent commendable efforts by people working in agencies that have juxtaposed or overlapping mandates. The arrangements are valuable for developing compatible policies and standards. However, questions arise as to effectiveness and efficiency of systems that require six or more separate national interagency coordinating bodies to agree on an action to be taken. Through multiple presentations, it was obvious to the panel that there is no clear, general understanding of the degree to which fire detection and initial attack are priorities. The unreconciled missions of various organizations result in a confusing diversity of efforts to suppress wildland fires. One issue presented to the panel with the strongest consensus was that a reduced emphasis on initial attack is harmful to the firefighting mission of land management agencies.

FINDING 5–CULTURE, ORGANIZATIONAL STRUCTURE, AND MANAGEMENT

The culture, organizational structure and management of federal wildland fire management agencies are ill suited to conduct safe and effective aviation operations in the current environment.

The panel saw the federal agencies' collective culture as the product of many years of professional attention to forest and other wildland management activities in conjunction with wildlife conservation. As the size and complexity of various agencies grew, so did a requirement to develop the skills and organizational structure needed to manage large organizations. Today, a coalition of agencies administers the federal aviation and ground firefighting programs. An examination of the joint structure would determine an appropriate balance of centralized and decentralized management. The panel notes that many large organizations operate well with centralized policy, standards, and funding control. Simultaneously, those organizations deliver services through a decentralized operations program that allows initiative and field-level discretion.

The apparent, but possibly illusory, reality that funding is never sufficient has bred a culture that accommodates risk in aerial firefighting activities. For the aviation program overall, this has translated to insufficient contract funding to provide adequate knowledge of aircraft condition; insufficient training, inspection, and maintenance; and a deplorable safety record for large air tankers. A culture that emphasizes cost-efficiency has also created an admirable, but hazardous, "can-do" ethos that pervades firefighting aviation.

Dedication to the professional aspects of land management has led to a patchwork of interagency committees that respect the mandates of partner organizations, but do not resolve basic aerial firefighting organizational and accountability issues. This has resulted in what was described to the panel as many forestry professionals in technical management positions that govern aviation programs. Regardless of their dedication, it is impossible for these managers to determine the technical requirements for a complex aviation program. The panel saw evidence of good leadership that would help to ensure effectiveness, efficiency, and safety in the federal aerial firefighting program. However, differing missions and incompatible organizational structures make any leader's task very difficult. It appeared to the panel that Forest Service and BLM leaders were not well versed on aircraft certification, airworthiness, and performance issues, nor their implications for flight safety.

FINDING 6–CERTIFICATION

The Federal Aviation Administration (FAA) has abrogated any responsibility to ensure the continued airworthiness of "public-use" aircraft, including ex-military aircraft converted to firefighting air tankers. Although these aircraft are awarded FAA type certificates, the associated certification processes do not require testing and inspection to ensure that the aircraft are airworthy to perform their intended missions.

The panel found that Forest Service and BLM leaders do not have a good understanding of the FAA's certification and oversight role regarding public-use aircraft. Additionally, they have placed an unjustifiable faith in the FAA's oversight of ex-military firefighting air tankers. Therefore, Forest Service and BLM personnel, contract operators, and aircrews are in the untenable position of having to determine whether an aircraft is safe to fly.

Under federal law, the FAA is responsible for ensuring that former military aircraft are approved for specialized operations, including firefighting. Once modified to an air tanker configuration, both civil and ex-military aircraft operate under a Restricted Category type certificate, which limits how they can be flown in the firefighting mission.

A Restricted Category type certificate governs how the aircraft is operated, and a Supplemental type certificate approves conversion modifications related to the firefighting mission, such as retardant tank installations. A Data Sheet accompanying the type certificate and Supplemental type certificate stipulates what records, manuals, military documents, and instructions for continued airworthiness must accompany the aircraft, according to the FAA presentation to the panel. FAA inspectors check air tanker operators' records to verify that operations are being conducted in accordance with regulations, but rarely, if ever, physically inspect an aircraft to ensure that it is safe to fly an intended mission.

The FAA's Restricted Category certification and continued airworthiness process also does not require the aircraft's Original Equipment Manufacturer to have any interaction with the current operator. Further, all ex-military aircraft historical records might be retained by the Department of Defense, not the manufacturer. Without engineering data and historical records, it is difficult to determine what inspections should be conducted and at what intervals. The situation also complicates development of maintenance and structural repair programs needed to ensure that an aircraft flying firefighting missions can be operated safely for an extended lifetime.

In the United States, air tanker operators having sufficient financial resources and engineering expertise might elect to inspect and repair their aircraft more frequently than required under military or civil transport maintenance plans to protect their investments and ensure flight crew safety. But there is no FAA requirement to do so, little or no FAA assistance or oversight, and the Forest Service does not contractually reward such extra measures.

FINDING 7–CONTRACTS

Government contracts for air tanker and helicopter fire management services do not adequately recognize business and operational realities or aircraft limitations. As a result, contract provisions contain disincentives to flight safety.

Federal agencies responsible for wildland aerial firefighting have adopted a widespread, short-term pursuit of cost-efficiency. A narrow cost-focus is evident in Forest Service and BLM contracts that do not reward value, performance, or safety. A lack of clear understanding about the long-term or life-cycle costs is evident in day-to-day fire-management decisions, safety-sensitive positions that remain vacant for extended periods, and asset-related decisions to save money.

The 2002 National Air tanker Service Contract requires adherence to federal regulations but does not require operators to conduct safe operations. Nothing in the contract requires contractors to operate their aircraft in accordance with maintenance and inspection schedules tailored to the known conditions of an aerial firefighting environment. The panel saw no evidence that contracting offices either knew about or had attempted to address known structural issues to ensure that contractor aircraft could be operated safely. The panel found nothing in the current air tanker contract that provided incentives for contractors to operate safely. Instead, contracts appear to rely on the FAA's Restricted Certificate of Airworthiness, which declares that an aircraft is "appropriate for use," and does little more than require that it be maintained in accordance with previous military criteria. Additionally, financial penalties assessed for periods when the aircraft are unavailable for service encourage contractors to fly aircraft that are not airworthy.

FINDING 8–TRAINING

Training is under funded and inadequately specified for helicopters, large air tankers, and other fixed-wing operations.

Presentations showed that, in general, aircrews of contract aircraft lack training in contemporary aviation management subjects. The Forest Service has not identified aircrew-training requirements, the contract award process does not consider aircrew-training accomplishments, nor are training records required as proof-of-accomplishment. There were no contract incentives found that would encourage operators to retain full time safety officers to supervise and manage aircrew training.

Aerial firefighters currently do not have an opportunity to fly together in a training environment. In particular, joint, integrated training of large air tanker and other fixed-wing crews is inadequate. Further, each element of the operation knows little about the others, except for what is learned during real-world operations. The panel saw that, quite unlike most professional aviation communities, air tanker pilots do not share information about successful techniques, good or bad results, and difficulties encountered in their operations. The panel was informed that current training does not develop civil firefighting capabilities, such as consistent drop accuracies backed by measures of operational effectiveness. Previous-season data are not used for sustainable, long-term improvements, either. Helicopter operations are similarly isolated from other air activities, and, from what the panel was told, helicopter crews learn little about the other elements of aerial firefighting, even when everyone is working over a wildland fire.

Background

For decades, the United States government has relied on aviation resources to fight forest fires, primarily in support of ground forces. Today, fixed-wing aircraft typically drop fire retardant to slow a fire's progress and give ground crews time to contain and extinguish a fire. A variety of helicopters carry water in suspended buckets to augment fixed-wing large air tankers and single-engine air tankers. Recently, large helicopters also have been fitted with onboard tanks and systems to increase the amount of water and retardant delivered.

This range of aircraft gives fire incident commanders a variety of airborne capabilities including:

- Large air tankers that fly hundreds of miles at 140 to 250+ knots and deliver up to 3,000 gallons of retardant, often to remote wildland fires.

- Single-engine air tankers that respond quickly to pop-up fires (initial attack) and carry about 800 gallons of retardant.

- Helicopters that provide high-accuracy delivery of water or retardant and minimal drop-and-return cycle times when there is a nearby water source.

Each aircraft type also has its strengths and limitations. Therefore, incident commanders and other firefighting professionals generally agree that all of the above aircraft types are needed to fight forest and rangeland blazes.

While today's firefighting aircraft have served federal agencies fairly well, recent fire seasons have exposed the seams and fault lines in an aging aircraft fleet, and its associated processes. Stressed air resources and a changing wildland environment have resulted in several fatal aerial firefighting accidents. During the 2002 fire season, two large, multiengine air tankers—a Lockheed C-130A Hercules and a Consolidated Vultee PB4Y-2 Privateer—suffered wing losses while they were delivering retardant. Five aircrew members died, victims of in-flight structural breakups. Then, an aging Aerospatiale SA 315B Lama helicopter suffered an engine failure and crashed, killing the pilot. Live media coverage brought the risks of aerial firefighting into living rooms across the nation, and increased awareness of a periodic problem with ex-military air tankers.

Introduction

In response to the 2002 fire season's fatal aircraft accidents, the USDA Forest Service and USDI Bureau of Land Management (BLM) jointly established an independent, five-member Blue Ribbon Commission (the panel—Appendix A) to identify essential information for planning a safe and effective future aviation program. On August 15, 2002, the Chief of the Forest Service and Director of the BLM asked the panel to identify weaknesses and fail points in the current aviation program, focusing on safety, operational effectiveness, costs, sustainability, and strategic guidance. Assuming an integrated approach, the agencies tasked the panel to address these five areas as they relate to the operation and supervision of air tankers, lead planes and air supervision modules, helicopters, and air attack platforms (Appeendix B).

Within a 90-day period, the panel held town hall meetings in Atlanta, Portland, Salt Lake City, Denver, Albuquerque, and Sacramento, soliciting comments and ideas from those having an interest in the federal firefighting aviation program. The Federal Aviation Administration, National Transportation Safety Board, California Department of Forestry and Fire Protection, and Canadian and United States air tanker operators, Conair and Aerounion, respectively, also provided special briefings to the panel. Verbal and written remarks were received from aerial firefighting-industry officials, air tanker contractors, aircraft manufacturers, fixed-wing and helicopter pilots, private-sector consultants, and concerned people. In addition, the panel heard commentary from representatives of state and federal agencies responsible for fighting wildland fires.

The panel has considered information received through presentations, field visits, and document reviews, such as government contracts. The massive amount of material and brief time for analysis forced the panel to address, for the most part, only major considerations. The panel relied significantly on the knowledge, experience, and judgment of its members to develop findings, which are strong inferences rather than deduced certainties.

The panel heard a consensus of many views, however, presenters also expressed clearly opposing views on certain subjects. The panel often discovered variation between the views conveyed and information contained in official documents. Many experienced professionals led the panel to accept their comments as sincere and representative of their perception of reality, which should not be neglected in favor of official documents.

Land management agencies, in general, have done an admirable job of executing their mandates to keep forests healthy, protect fisheries, and ensure that national parks are available for public enjoyment by relying on the professional and technical competencies of dedicated employees. *Possibly the single largest challenge now facing leaders of these federal agencies is to foster cooperation and collaboration among working-level staffs, contractors, and states to raise the standards of aerial wildland firefighting in the United States.*

The panel interpreted the Forest Service and BLM decision to commission an independent review as agency recognition that fundamental aerial firefighting program changes are needed, and that an external perspective was necessary to help identify elements contributing to those changes. To avoid any conflict of interest or perception of influence, there was limited contact between the panel and top-level managers of the Forest Service and BLM. A list of selected panel presentations and communications (Appendix C) and references (Appendix D) are included as appendices to this report.

This report presents eight key findings (Table 1), which the panel believes are critical for planning a safe and effective future firefighting aviation program. The panel's mandate was to identify problems, not advocate solutions or make recommendations.

FINDING 1–SAFETY

The safety record of fixed-wing aircraft and helicopters used in federal wildland fire management is unacceptable.

FINDING 2–NEW ENVIRONMENT, NEW RISKS

Because the wildland environment has changed significantly, controlling wildland fires cannot be considered an auxiliary mission second to land management. Wildland firefighting has grown to a level of importance that warrants the attention of national leaders.

FINDING 3–AIRCRAFT

Under the current system of aircraft certification, contracting, and operation, key elements of the aerial wildland firefighting fleet are unsustainable.

FINDING 4–MISSION

The variety of missions, philosophies, and unclear standards of federal land management agencies creates a "mission muddle" that seriously compromises the safety and effectiveness of aviation in wildland fire management.

FINDING 5–CULTURE, ORGANIZATIONAL STRUCTURE AND MANAGEMENT

The culture, organizational structure and management of federal wildland fire management agencies are ill suited to conduct safe and effective aviation operations in the current environment.

FINDING 6–CERTIFICATION

The Federal Aviation Administration (FAA) has abrogated any responsibility to ensure the continued airworthiness of "public-use" aircraft, including ex-military aircraft converted to firefighting air tankers. Although these aircraft are awarded FAA type certificates, the associated certification processes do not require testing and inspection to ensure that the aircraft are airworthy to perform their intended missions.

FINDING 7–CONTRACTS

Government contracts for air tanker and helicopter fire management services do not adequately recognize business and operational realities or aircraft limitations. As a result, contract provisions contain disincentives to flight safety.

FINDING 8–TRAINING

Training is under funded and inadequately specified for helicopters, large air tankers, and other fixed-wing operations.

Table 1. Overview of the key findings of the Blue Ribbon Panel on aviation in relation to the five areas chartered for determination of adequacy in the current federal aviation system.

Findings	Safety	Operational Effectiveness	Cost	Sustainability	Strategic Guidance
1. Safety	X			X	
2. New Environment, New Risks					X
3. Aircraft	X			X	
4. Mission		X			X
5. Culture Organizational, Structure, and Management		X	X		X
6. Certification	X			X	
7. Contracts			X		
8. Training	X	X			

FINDING 1–SAFETY

The safety record of fixed-wing aircraft and helicopters used in wildland fire management is unacceptable.

Although selected data indicate there is a general, long-term improvement in accident rates, the aerial firefighting community acknowledged to the panel that its safety record is abysmal. A historical review showed that 136 large air tanker crew members have died in aircraft accidents since 1958. As a comparative illustration, if ground firefighters had the same fatality rate, they would have suffered more than 200 on-the-job deaths per year. When 14 firefighters were killed in the 1994 Storm King Mountain tragedy, the incident triggered massive changes in ground firefighting strategies and practices to improve safety. There has been no comparable government response to aerial firefighter fatalities.

During its review, the panel was told that safety-related strategy changes were transferring firefighting risks from ground crews to air operations, which compounds the situation. The Forest Service's Rocky Mountain Region 2 *Large Fire Review* completed in August 2002 notes that, "Mitigating the risk to ground firefighters by using aviation resources can be effective, as long as the decisions are made with an understanding that this will typically increase the risks to aviation."

An indication that the federal government is starting to embrace and insist upon safety as a priority was taken in 1996 when the National Transportation Safety Board assumed responsibility for investigating serious aerial firefighting accidents. This move represented significant progress toward safer operations because, in the past, land management agencies had to conduct their own investigations of aircraft incidents. Managers are striving to provide the leadership that ensures all employees and contractors place the highest value on safety. Effective safety programs have proven cost effective.

Although safety is continually emphasized during wildland firefighting operations, instructions for government agencies, such as the Forest Service and BLM, which investigate aviation accidents in-house, are focused on process compliance. Other segments of the aviation industry have found that, to improve safety through accident investigation, procedures must be non punitive, and provide incentives for willing and expeditious information disclosure.

Large, Fixed-wing Air Tankers

The panel determined that contractor personnel flying large air tankers are subject to a lower safety standard than government personnel flying federally owned and operated lead planes and smoke-jumper aircraft. Further, the level of safety for both contractor and government aerial firefighting operations is lower than can be financially justified, and is less than expected for any employer concerned about its employees. In other words, the federal government is asking employees involved in aerial firefighting to take unnecessary risks. However, it expects contractor crew members to assume an even higher degree of risk than government employees.

This disparity in safety standards stems from a government contracting process that assumes the airworthiness of today's large air tanker fleet has been assured by the FAA's type certification process (See Finding 6 - Certification). In fact, responsibility for the continued airworthiness of aircraft converted to air tankers is up to the contractors who own and operate the aging aircrafts. Since aerial firefighting subjects structures and engines to more severe stresses than those experienced when flying the civil or military missions for which these aircraft were originally designed, air tanker contracts cannot simply insist that a contractor ensure safe operations. Contract clauses cannot and do not offset either the absence of FAA oversight or the more demanding operating conditions. As a result, large air tanker contracts do not provide for sufficient maintenance, continued airworthiness, and the training necessary to ensure safe operations. Funding for the aerial firefighting program appears to be either inadequate or ineffectively distributed.

Historically, the federally contracted large air tanker fleet of about 41 aircraft has lost an average of one tanker each year to flying accidents; many involved fatalities. In 2002—a season of particularly heavy firefighting activity—two in-flight breakups resulted in the indefinite grounding of 11 large air tankers, because their airworthiness was suspect. This represented approximately one-quarter of the fleet.

The remaining ex-military large air tanker fleet is probably at risk of being withdrawn from future operations, unless a major investment is made in testing, inspection, and maintenance to ensure airworthiness. One expert told the panel that, from an engineering perspective, there is no assurance that any of the old military aircraft currently in operation are safe to fly as air tankers. Modern engineering techniques, such as damage tolerance analyses, are not being widely used to predict the likelihood of the continued airworthiness of the entire aerial firefighting fleet, which includes large air tankers, single-engine tankers, lead planes, helicopters, and smoke-jumper aircraft.

A safe, effective aviation program depends upon acquiring improved aerial firefighting resources, then ensuring that they are maintained to a high safety standard;

precedents for such a transformation exist in this community. Through interviews with Canadian operator Conair, the panel learned that the company had made significant improvements in its safety record by establishing a safety department, revising inspection and maintenance programs, and introducing a comprehensive training regimen. Conair modeled its safety program after one initiated by Petroleum Helicopters, Inc., which supports offshore oil-drilling operations in the Gulf of Mexico. The Canadian operator now claims 60,000 accident-free flight hours in support of fire suppression.

Helicopters

The panel saw no reports that identified in-flight structural failures or break-ups of helicopters. However, in reviewing a document that summarized 36 aviation accidents related to fire service helicopters during the past 10 years, many accidents had similar features. Almost one-third of the reviewed accidents related to mechanical failure, approximately one-quarter were associated with operating at the edge of or outside the approved flight envelope, and clusters of accidents involved entanglements with loads or long-lines. Several wire-strike incidents also were noted. The high accident rate appears to be associated with deficiencies in operational control, maintenance, and training.

The panel also found that varying airworthiness standards required under federal firefighting contracts had an impact on helicopter safety. Many types of helicopters are covered by either Air Carrier or Standard FAA airworthiness certification criteria, which are generally associated with airlines and general aviation, respectively. If not widely used for these purposes, large helicopters are operated with a Restricted Type certificate of airworthiness, which is based on the last known military or commercial use. However, when flown as public-use aircraft, such as during aerial firefighting activities, the "operations are exempt from most FAA oversight," according to an FAA briefing provided to the panel. Still, much of the helicopter work associated with firefighting is consistent with the helicopter's original mission design.

Federal firefighting helicopters in the United States are not required to have voice or data recorders installed. In contrast, voice recorders are standard equipment on most helicopters in the United Kingdom. Additionally, U.K. helicopters have microphones installed at the rotor mast to sense mechanical sounds, which provides an effective and inexpensive tool to analyze mechanical failures during accident investigations.

Lead Planes

The Forest Service owns and operates a fleet of 19 pressurized Beechcraft Baron BE-58P aircraft. Although flown in a variety of roles, the Barons' principal mission is to serve as lead planes for large air tankers, guiding the heavy aircraft to retardant drop areas. Air tanker pilots consider lead planes a significant safety enhancement and, at times, will refuse a retardant delivery run unless a lead plane has checked the area for escape routes, obstacles, and adequate maneuverability. A Forest Service pilot told the panel that although initial attack of a fire is possible without a lead plane, when doing so, air tanker crews "are operating with the safety net removed."

One reason the Baron was selected for the lead plane role is because it has two engines, which enables a pilot to return safely to an airport if one engine fails or is shut down in-flight. However, the Baron has a single-engine service ceiling of about 7,300 feet when weighing 5,500 pounds and flying in standard-day air temperature (59 °F and pressure of 29.92 inches of mercury), and standard barometric pressure conditions, according to Raytheon Aircraft's 2001 Baron 58 Performance/Specifications.

Many lead plane missions are flown over mountainous terrain during summer months when temperatures are well above those of a standard day. Under these conditions, air density is much lower than at sea level, which reduces the capability of an aircraft to maintain altitude. In addition, much of the terrain in fire-prone regions, particularly in the western United States, is higher than the Baron's single-engine service ceiling, which is the maximum altitude that a multiengine aircraft can maintain a 50-foot/minute rate of climb when flying on one engine. The panel spoke to several pilots from Denver, Albuquerque, and Boise that fly Barons in areas where single-engine performance is often inadequate due to high altitudes and temperatures. They admitted that they knowingly flew many missions over terrain where Barons will not stay airborne with only one engine functioning. Although government decision makers also are aware of this situation, managers still assign lead plane missions into these areas, and pilots accept the missions because, as the panel was told, "If we don't (fly in these conditions), someone else will." The panel believes that it is unjustifiable to place Baron crews at risk in regions where the single-engine performance of their aircraft is inadequate to ensure crew and passenger safety.

The Baron fleet is also experiencing a high rate of maintenance problems, raising concerns about the long-term sustainability of safe operations. Pilots in two Forest Service regions reported that, of the approximately 10 Barons available to them during the 2002 fire season, two sustained engine fires, one had a severe fuel leak, two experienced engine failures, and one sustained permanent wing-skin deformity due to overstress. They also said that, "the Barons are only ready for service about half the time."

The structural life expectancy for Barons flying the firefighting mission also is questionable (See Finding 3 - Aircraft). At this point, it would appear that Baron operations cannot be easily limited to missions that can be conducted safely, and there are no other suitable aircraft available to assume firefighting functions. Attempts have been made to identify suitable replacements for the aging, performance-limited Baron fleet. For example, in a 1999 validation of aircraft performance-solution criteria used in the interagency National Study of Tactical Aerial Resource Management to Support Initial Attack and Large Fire Suppression, the Aviation Management Council called for a higher-performance aircraft to replace the Barons. The council said that the replacement aircraft should have a single-engine service ceiling of 10,000 feet when flying at gross-allowable weight on a day when temperatures were 30 °F above the standard-day conditions (89 °F), have visibility that is equivalent to or better than that of the Baron, be capable of good maneuverability, and be able to operate safely on one engine throughout the required lead plane flight regime.

Flight Data/Cockpit Voice Recorders

Damage-resistant voice and data recorders on aircraft are essential for effective accident investigations. However, no Forest Service or BLM policy requires recorders to be installed on either government-owned or contractor-flown aircraft. The cockpit voice recorder is a relatively inexpensive addition, and it can provide valuable information. In addition to registering the crew's voices, the recorder documents various aircraft sounds that can be used effectively in accident investigations. Flight data recorders are more expensive and require installation of transducers throughout an aircraft. Quick-access recorders that monitor the physical condition of an aircraft during long periods are also available. Although any of these recorders could be installed during scheduled heavy maintenance checks, Forest Service contracts do not provide for them.

FINDING 2–NEW ENVIRONMENT, NEW RISKS

Because the wildland environment has changed significantly, controlling wildland fires cannot be considered an auxiliary mission secondary to land management. Wildland firefighting has grown to a level of importance that warrants the attention of national leaders.

America's wildland fire protection policies were established after the nation suffered catastrophic life and property losses during the massive fires of the 1800s and early 1900s. The tragic 1871 Peshtigo fire in Wisconsin and Michigan claimed more than 1,500 lives and consumed 3.7 million acres. In 1902, the Yacoult Fire in Washington burned more than 1 million acres and killed 38 people. The Great Idaho or "Big Blowup" fire in 1910 consumed 3 million acres and took another 85 lives, leading to "a call for a systemic policy change. Less than a year [after the Idaho fire], the national Forest Service firefighting program was born, and a war on all wildfires was declared. From that point on, all wildfires were extinguished as soon as possible," according to *A Report to the President In Response to the Wildfires of 2000.*

The Weeks Act of 1911 and the Clark-McNary act of 1924 authorized federal spending for cooperative fire-control programs with the states. During World War I, the new policies took on a national security perspective when leaders feared enemy saboteurs could easily start hundreds of massive wildland fires, overwhelming the country's firefighting capabilities.

With a few exceptions, the revised program reduced the number of large fires experienced by the United States during the 20th century. However, nature's pattern of periodic cleansing fires was interrupted and the forests became overgrown. According to the 2000 Report to the President: "While the policy of aggressive fire suppression appeared to be successful, it set the stage for the intense fires that we see today. Full suppression of all wildland fires initially gave our forests and wildlands a chance to heal, creating a false sense of security. However, after many years of suppressing fires, thus disrupting normal ecological cycles, changes in the structure and makeup of forests began to occur. Species of trees that ordinarily would have been eliminated from forests by periodic, low-intensity fires began to become a dominant part of the forest canopy. Over time, these trees became susceptible to insects and disease. Standing dead and dying trees, in conjunction with other brush and downed material, began to fill the forest floor. The resulting accumulation of these materials, when dried by extended periods of drought, created the fuels that promote the type of wildfires that we have seen this year [2000]."

Fuels Plus Drought

Much of the nation has been subjected to prolonged and severe drought since 1996, which has created, in some areas, the worst fire danger experienced in more than 100 years. Forest Service data indicate that as of October 2002 nearly 50% of the United States landmass "continues to be in a moderate-to-extreme state of drought." The agency's forecasters said that the drought conditions are expected for at least another 3 to 4 years.

This altered environment, and its associated risks, manifested in 1998 when Texas and Florida experienced 6 of the 10 largest wildland fires in the nation. An escaped prescribed burn in 2000 was a national wake-up call that highlighted how dangerous wildland fires could quickly become under drought conditions. The Cerro Grande fire destroyed 235 homes and damaged many others in Los Alamos, New Mexico, and forced 18,000 people to evacuate. The fire burned almost 48,000 acres and threatened Los Alamos National Laboratory, one of the nation's nuclear weapons design facilities.

Fires consumed 8.4 million acres of United States wildland in 2000, and 6.8 million acres burned in 2002, which is nearly double the 10-year average. Two fires characterized by Forest Service officials as "super fires" in 2002 blackened up to half a million acres each. The nation's wildland firefighters managed to catch and extinguish 98% to 99% of all blazes. Still, the remaining large fires caused tremendous damage, cost millions of dollars to fight, and will require the expenditure of significant additional funds to reconstitute burn areas, protect watersheds, and prevent erosion and flooding.

Wildland-urban Interface

The panel was told that today's complex, high-risk wildland fire environment differs considerably from what existed a few decades ago. Shifting population patterns have complicated the challenges faced by professional firefighters. In the mid 1900s, most wildland fires occurred in remote forests and rangelands, where they rarely threatened people and structures. Fire managers could either commit resources and fight a fire or allow it burn, depending on their assessment of risk to lives and property.

Development of a wildland-urban interface (an area where structures and other human development meet or intermingle with undeveloped wildland or vegetative fuels) has forced today's managers to contend with entirely different options. People are increasingly moving into rural areas, building homes, ranchettes, summer cabins, condominium complexes, and communities in and adjacent to public lands. Significantly different firefighting philosophies and tactics are required when fires threaten developed areas. Additionally, the associated risks and costs of protecting people and structures in these areas are skyrocketing, according to officials at the National Interagency Fire Center.

For example, by early September 2002, the Sour Biscuit Fire in Oregon had burned more than 500,000 acres, destroyed 13 structures, and cost about $100 million to fight. A fire that large in many other areas of the nation could have destroyed hundreds, might be thousands of homes, adding billions of dollars to the loss column. In Oregon, Arizona, and Colorado, an unusually large number of ground and aerial firefighting resources were assigned to protect small towns and housing enclaves during the 2002 fire season. Almost all firefighting efforts were successful, thanks to heroic firefighter efforts and good luck. But these were costly campaigns. One Forest Service firefighter in Boise told the panel, "We could have bought [one] entire town for what we spent protecting it." Under current wildland firefighting rules, firefighters cannot distinguish between the value of an old barn and a new million-dollar home; both must be protected.

Demands Versus Aerial Firefighting Capabilities

Forest Service and BLM aviation resources traditionally committed to aerial fire support, mitigation, control, and suppression are no longer equal to the growing threat presented by the confluence of complex factors. Demanding firefighting challenges in the wildland-urban interface, in particular, require more and better equipment, new strategies, and increased coordination among local, state, and federal agencies. The latter situation has increased the complexity of deciding who has responsibility for a fire, and what resources should be allocated. For example, while federal and state agencies are primarily responsible for forest firefighting, state, local, and volunteer fire organizations are charged with protecting structures. When a fire occurs in the wildland-urban interface where several parties appear to have jurisdiction, it is often unclear who should be in charge and who should pay for air resources.

Recently, large fires have had a major impact on Forest Service and BLM aviation resources. In 2002, every available large air tanker was brought on-contract up to 45 days early, and most of the aircraft flew about twice as many hours as they would in a typical year. Many Forest Service officials that spoke to the panel said that this will become standard practice rather than the exception over the next 10 to 15 years. In the 1980s, "when a tanker reached 100 flight hours in a season, it was a major occasion. Two hundred hours was extremely rare," a Forest Service lead plane pilot said. In the 1990s, air tankers averaged 250 to 400 hours each season, and the trend toward 400-hour years has continued.

Longer, more active fire seasons characterized by wildland fires that burn up to 500,000 acres stress aircraft and engines to unprecedented levels, which increases maintenance demands. The aging large air tanker fleet was supposed to focus on initial attack missions, but instead it has become a standard tool for fighting large fires, which further aggravates airframe and engine degradation. Concerns over rapidly growing wing cracks were quickly elevated when two air tankers suffered wing losses and crashed last summer. Large air tankers also fly more missions when battling large fires, and the associated stresses take a heavy toll on the limited number of aircraft, engines, pilots, maintenance technicians, and other support personnel. If the nation continues to experience large wildland fires, Forest Service employees told the panel, the situation will only get worse.

A National Problem

There has never been a comprehensive, national-level reevaluation of federal aerial firefighting, involving professional aerial firefighting personnel in developing effective concepts and strategies in the United States. If the United States Congress, administration, and federal agencies responsible for protecting lives and property continue with the current approach to fighting wildland fire, there is a high probability that supplementary appropriations will be required in most years. There is an equal probability that lives and property will be subjected to unacceptable risks and costs associated with wildland fires.

National leaders' awareness of, and interest in, wildland firefighting usually diminishes after a fire season, as other issues demand their attention. The 2002 season might be different, though. High-profile fires in Arizona, Colorado and Oregon, punctuated by the tragic losses of air tankers, helicopters, flight crews, and ground firefighters, should help to ensure long-term public interest. The panel believes that people in the United States are expecting national-level attention and significant changes to prevent needless air tanker crashes and mitigate large fires.

The United States currently does not have an aviation plan rooted in zero-tolerance for wildland fire disasters and backed by a full-time national cadre of aerial firefighting professionals ready to respond to a wave of large fires. The panel did not receive suggestions that any of the large 2002 fires might be attributed to terrorism, but today's volatile wildland environment is clearly vulnerable to such a threat. Forest Service managers told the panel that it was simply lucky that a series of large fires was not intentionally ignited simultaneously during the 2002 fire season, and expressed concern that the nation might not be as fortunate in the future. A March 2000 USDA Inspector General's audit report (08001-2-HQ) began with the comment, "Recent terrorist acts in this country underscore the importance of security over the Department's infrastructure. Further, no top-level action to anticipate, prevent and, if necessary, quickly suppress human-ignited fires appears to be necessary." But that was before the September 11, 2001, attacks on New York and Washington changed the national security environment and introduced new risks. People in the United States expect to be protected from any number of threats now, including loss of life and property from human-ignited wildland fires.

The environmental conditions that created today's threat of large fires have taken decades to develop and are not the fault of any political party or federal land management agency. The conditions evolved from uncoordinated policy changes that responded largely to public demands and have been exacerbated by shifting demographics, severe drought, and a drastic change in the national security landscape. The situation has the potential to become a collective national problem that begs for correction.

FINDING 3–AIRCRAFT

Under the current system of aircraft certification, contracting, and operation, key elements of the aerial wildland firefighting fleet are unsustainable.

Using aircraft to fight forest fires has grown from the visionary application of technology that brought air vehicles into many of today's activities. Initially, small agricultural aircraft fitted with tanks for applying chemicals were modified to drop water and retardant. Later, larger single-engine, mostly ex-military aircraft that had been converted for use in aerial pest control, were introduced to firefighting. Their success led to a search for even larger aircraft that could carry more retardant. For years, many World

War II-vintage aircraft, such as B-25s, A-26s and the PBY Catalina, were used. The usefulness of large aircraft was apparent, leading to acquisition and conversion to air tanker of "newer" surplus military aircraft, such as the C-119 Flying Boxcar.

Recognizing that the acquisition and operation of aircraft were new specialties, federal land management agencies established several organizations to administer these elements. An Interagency Airtanker Board was created to oversee aircraft requirements and the installation of tank systems that carry and deliver retardant. Having limited background in civil aviation, the board relied heavily on the FAA's aircraft type-certification process. However, the panel did not see indications that the Interagency Airtanker Board fully understands the implications of operating under FAA Restricted Category type certificates. The board occasionally saw that some aspects of airworthiness were not receiving adequate attention, forcing it to assume certain roles usually reserved for an airworthiness authority.

This generation of aircraft was used successfully until it began to have wing failures and was retired. The industry then turned to larger and more modern P-2Vs and C-130As, which provided increased capability. These were used successfully until the 2002 fire season, when two large air tankers, a World War II-vintage PB4Y and an aging, but more modern, turbo-propeller-powered C-130A, broke-up in flight, killing their crews. Shortly thereafter, the Forest Service withdrew both of these aircraft types from the large air tanker fleet.

Predictable Cycle

Recent in-flight structural failures signaled the recurrence of a problem that has periodically plagued firefighting air tankers for half a century. This is the end of a third type of aircraft cycle, which have each culminated in accidents and crew fatalities. Each cycle begins with the Forest Service and its private-sector contractors obtaining retired military bombers, transports, and patrol aircraft from the Pentagon's "boneyard." Stripping-out unneeded systems to reduce weight, contractors outfit the air tankers with fire retardant tanks and delivery systems, obtain FAA Restricted Category type certificates, and put the aircraft into firefighting service. There are a few nonmilitary exceptions, such as FAA-certified commercial air transports converted to air tankers, but, to the panel's knowledge, none of these have suffered catastrophic structural failures.

Large air tankers, operated for 15 to 20 years by private companies under contract to the Forest Service, experience varying degrees of engine, systems, and structural problems. To date, each approximately 20-year cycle has ended with fatal accidents, which are often attributed to structural failures. The panel was told that, over the last 50 years or so, B-17s, C-119s, PB4Ys and C-130As have experienced in-flight structural failures, while one C-119 and two PB4Ys landed safely with major structural damage, but never flew again.

During the 2002 fire season, the predictable result of a large air tanker system based on a "good enough" contracting philosophy and strategy materialized again. But, in the panel's view, the fatal air tanker crashes this year were predictable. For several reasons, the federal government has repeatedly opted for old aircraft retired by the military services. They were inexpensive, they were available and, for the most part, their earlier use had involved the capability to drop weapons or cargo from the air. However, the panel was told by a Forest Service official that, "We use them because they're cheap." The panel learned that the aerial firefighting industry is running out of spare parts for these old aircraft, and is often manufacturing its own replacements. Presenters told the panel that obtaining 100-octane aviation fuel and the right type of oil for radial engines is becoming more difficult.

Low-Cost Paradigm

Private operators, for the most part, have done an admirable job of keeping these aging aircraft flying. However, they are handicapped by receiving little, if any, support from former military operators and the aircraft's original manufacturer. Smaller contractors have minimal in-house engineering capability. Additionally, the FAA has essentially said, "It's a public-use aircraft. You're on your own."

The Forest Service, as the government contracting authority, opted for a system that provided the least expensive aircraft capable of delivering fire retardant. While calling these contracts "value-based," the agency appears to heavily weight its contractor-selection in favor of price.

These factors have fostered an atmosphere characterized by minimal levels of safety and reliability, but an expectation of sustained performance. Millions of dollars are spent each year to keep 40 to 46 large air tankers on-contract and available for firefighting. However, there are few checks and balances to ensure that the aircraft are airworthy and safe to fly throughout a fire season. Additionally, contractors have no financial incentive and are not required to ensure that their aircraft are safe to fly. A low contractual standard for ensuring the safety of large air tankers through strong inspection and maintenance programs might financially penalize, at least in the short run, more conscientious operators who choose to maintain a higher safety standard.

Turning Point

In 2002, the laws of probability caught up with the federal contracting system and five large air tanker airmen died. Safety concerns forced the Forest Service to ground about a quarter of the large air tanker fleet, further straining firefighting resources and costing the agency millions of dollars. Grounding the C-130As cost the agency $1.2 million, the panel was told. In short, the seams and fault lines of a complex, once-acceptable, cost-driven aerial firefighting system were exposed by the 2002 fire season. There are many contributing reasons, and this report identifies a number of them. However, questions remain: What can and should be done about an aged large air tanker fleet before the next fire season? How can the Forest Service, BLM, and other government agencies ensure that the existing air tanker fleet can operate safely and effectively? The panel heard opinions from a broad spectrum of people and organizations that have a stake in aerial firefighting. But those opinions were backed by few verifiable facts and technical data. The panel heard that:

- The air tanker fleet is "tired and worn out."

- Given enough money, operators can inspect, repair, and put safe aircraft back in service next year.

- Old air tankers should be replaced by newer ex-military aircraft, specifically, C-130B/E/Hs and P-3Bs.

- Reengineering and strengthening the structures of existing aircraft would suffice.

- Heavy-lift helicopters and a fleet of single-engine air tankers can do the job as well as large air tankers.

- New aircraft tailored for the firefighting role is the answer.

A common thread was a concern about costs. A number of potentially viable options appeared to be routinely dismissed as too expensive before being carefully examined, perhaps reflecting this community's "no-money" state-of-mind. The panel was told that both government employees and contractors assume that Congress, the administration, and federal agencies will never provide the money needed to do the firefighting job correctly and safely, leaving them to manage with whatever Forest Service and BLM budgets allow.

Large Air Tanker Operating Environment

The panel recognized that a systems-level approach is needed to improve the current large air tanker situation. To better understand the system-wide environment in which air tankers operate, the panel asked the Forest Service and BLM to allow one or two of its members to fly on an air tanker or lead plane over an active fire. Forest Service and BLM officials, due to a restriction on carrying non-crew members in operational aircraft, denied the requests. Consequently, the panel relied entirely on presentations and reports to make environmental assessments, particularly concerning the levels of turbulence and maneuvering loads that large air tankers experience. Some respondents said turbulence ranged from moderate to severe levels. One said that maneuvering loads were typically less than 2 gs, "about like you'd see during a missed approach."

The panel sought technical information that would quantify the actual stresses large air tankers are subjected to when fighting a fire, particularly in mountainous terrain, however, little data were available. The most telling data came from a 1974 NASA Langley Research Center report, *Operating Experiences of Retardant Bombers During Firefighting Operations*. The report summarized findings from two well-instrumented Douglas DC-6B air tankers that flew 415 flights and made 1,175 retardant drops in the northwestern mountains of the United States during two fire seasons. The report indicated that flight loads and maneuver aggressiveness actually experienced by the DC-6Bs exceeded pilot estimates. Some report findings and excerpts follow:

- The DC-6B's design maneuver limit load factor (the maximum normal acceleration, measured in gs, that an aircraft is expected to experience in service) "was equaled or exceeded during recovery from 10 percent of the retardant drops. The ultimate load factor was exceeded once." Ultimate load factor is a limit load multiplied by a prescribed factor of safety, typically 1.5 for FAA-certified transports, and is usually never reached in aircraft service. The DC-6B that exceeded the ultimate load factor was maneuvering to avoid hitting a canyon wall obscured by smoke. "No visible structural damage was detected . . . [and] was probably due to the fact that the airplane was well below the maximum gross weight, since two retardant drops had been made prior to the incident."

- The loads experienced by DC-6Bs in the firefighting role far exceeded those a DC-6 would ever experience in its FAA-certified mission, which is to transport passengers and cargo. The report said, "The rate that maneuver load factors between 2.0 and 2.4 were experienced by firefighting aircraft was almost 1,000 times that for aircraft flown as commercial transports. The severity of maneuver load applications, in both magnitude and frequency of occurrence, is such that significant shortening of the structural life of the aircraft should be expected."

- Rates of descent during retardant-drop runs ranged from zero for flat approaches to 9,000 feet/minute during steep approaches in canyons or along canyon walls. The latter figure is comparable to what a military fighter, such as an F-16, might achieve during a steep-angle bomb delivery. The report said, "Based on data . . . it was calculated that 30 percent of the runs made by retardant bombers in mountainous areas can be expected to equal or exceed rates of descent of 3,000 feet per minute." Pullout load factors on the aircraft during retardant drops and recoveries ranged from -0.5 g to 3.9 g.

The NASA report's observations about flight parameters were replicated in the *1983 Operational Retardant Evaluation Study* (Fire Suppression Research Report 1990). This study collected data from seven large air tankers from 1983 to 1989, and showed that average drop speeds exceeded maximum-allowed drop speeds. Acceleration limits were exceeded on 20% of the drops, and 4 gs were exceeded an average of once every hundred drops.

During the 2002 fire season, after the two tragic wing-loss accidents, one Forest Service large air tanker operator contracted with American AeroStructures LLC of Colorado Springs, CO, to assess the structural integrity of its P-2V air tankers. The entire P-2V fleet was experiencing rapid wing-crack initiation and propagation. Inspectors found one aircraft had a 13-inch wing crack. On another, a crack grew 5 inches during one day of firefighting. Key findings recounted by American AeroStructures engineers during a presentation to the panel included:

- "Currently, no engineering basis exists to assume the existing [large air tanker] fleet is safe to fly today, much less in years to come," said K. Dale Roberts, an FAA Structures Designated Engineering Representative.

- Pilots routinely exceed g-limits during pullouts after dropping fire retardant. In one case, a P-2V pilot hit the aircraft's maximum g-limit on four of seven missions in a single day.

- The firefighting mission, especially in mountainous terrain, forces pilots to routinely exceed g-limits that large air tanker aircraft usually would not expect to reach but a few times in the aircraft's life.

- All large air tankers are experiencing rapid structural aging, accentuated by routine overloading. For example, about 80% of P-3 Orions have experienced wing-cracking problems and might not be structurally qualified to carry a 3,000-

gallon retardant tank, although they currently are FAA-certified to do so. Wings might be significantly overloaded when carrying a full retardant load, based on weight limits imposed by the United States Navy, which operates P-3s.

- All large air tankers are now at risk of catastrophic in-flight structural failure, because none of the aircraft have been properly analyzed and inspected to determine how fast their structures are deteriorating. Further, none of the ex-military large air tankers have been properly instrumented with accelerometers, strain gages, recorders, etc. to document the actual environment they are subjected to while firefighting.

- The firefighting mission differs significantly from the transport and patrol missions that the current ex-military air tanker fleet was designed to perform. The aircraft were not designed for firefighting, which is a more severe flight environment than carrying and delivering cargo. (This point was vigorously disputed by air tanker operators during panel presentations. However, the panel was unable to locate any data to substantiate operator claims that the firefighting load spectrum is equivalent to that experienced during the military missions for which these aircraft were designed. The previously discussed 1974 NASA study and the *Operational Retardant Evaluation (ORE) Study Status Report* would appear to undermine operator claims.)

Expert Opinion

None of the following potential strategic options from engineering and firefighting experts are part of today's Forest Service or BLM aerial firefighting programs. During the next several years, the large air tanker fleet could continue to operate if guided by a FAA-approved proactive, comprehensive structural inspection/repair program based on rigorous damage tolerance analyses tailored to the firefighting mission. This would require instrumenting an aircraft of each type in the fleet with enough sensors and recorders to characterize the aerial firefighting environment, thus providing a solid, known baseline for analyses and initiation of a Structural Life Extension Program. An estimate provided by American AeroStructures suggests that the required analysis and evaluation would cost approximately $400,000 to $600,000 per aircraft type; actual mitigation efforts and repairs would add an unknown cost per aircraft. This program would involve analyses and flight data that could identify any structural components and systems that might be aging faster than expected. With FAA oversight and participation, each aircraft type would adhere to a large air tanker inspection schedule based on an accelerated-life formula similar to that required by Canadian authorities.

Stragetic options include:

- Where engineering analyses and testing deem it necessary, wing skins might be replaced with modern types of metal. American AeroStructures officials noted that the C-130A and P-2V, for example, were built with metals that, under today's design practices, would not be suitable for aircraft structures.

- A structurally upgraded, FAA-certified large air tanker fleet might remain in service longer if it were limited to aggressive, timely initial fire attacks. The panel was told that large air tankers are routinely used for retardant deliveries on extended and large fires, although conventional firefighting wisdom indicates they are most effective in an initial attack role. Large air tankers are sometimes used where they are not particularly effective because people, news media, and public officials equate fire bombers dropping retardant with aggressive firefighting, the panel was told. Unless they see large air tankers flying overhead, "people don't think you're really fighting a big fire," one Forest Service official said. This "public relations factor" is not the best use of limited large air tanker resources, and exposes flight crews to unnecessary risks, he added.

- To ensure flight crew safety, large air tanker operations might be limited to aircraft that have been inspected and repaired by FAA-certified repair stations, ideally with third-party engineering support.

- Evaluations of leased purpose-built aircraft, such as the Russian Be-200 amphibian, could help identify mid- and long-term candidates for modernizing the air tanker fleet. Several presenters suggested that the A-10 Thunderbolt II or "Warthog," modified for aerial firefighting, could be a viable candidate. The A-10 was designed to operate in a close-air support role, which is somewhat analogous to fire retardant delivery. However, it is unlikely that the Department of Defense would provide any A-10 aircraft for evaluation in this role, based on its current stance on releasing retired military aircraft.

Although the recommendations of the comprehensive *National Study of Air Tankers to Support Initial Attack and Large Fire Suppression* were valid in the 1990s, events have shifted the bases upon which it was founded, rendering the conclusions moot. Its authors recommended that the Department of Defense provide newer ex-military aircraft, but the Pentagon is clearly not inclined to provide those aircraft, saying they are needed for national security purposes. The aircraft simply are not available for transfer, the Department of Defense maintains.

The panel believes obtaining and outfitting newer military aircraft, such as C-130s and P-3s, would only perpetuate a cycle that has proven to be unsustainable and dangerous. Unless the FAA and operator community change its methods, one could expect to see another cycle of structural failures and pilot fatalities within a decade or two. This strongly suggests that it is time to abandon what the panel considers a 50-year-old unsustainable strategy.

The panel heard presentations indicating that it is currently possible to develop a fleet of purpose-built, turbine-engine, fixed-wing air tankers based on well-defined requirements. Air Tractor, Inc. and Pyronautics, Inc. presented concepts for multiengine air tankers designed specifically for the aerial firefighting environment. The companies suggested that they would be interested in developing such aircraft if the federal government sought credible proposals, and backed them with contracts compatible with sound business acumen. Some proposed that because the Forest Service and Department of Interior agencies are not well suited to conduct an aircraft acquisition program, they might consider using an "executive agent" to handle everything from contracting to aircraft flight testing and production. The panel notes that the Department of Defense has established a workable precedent. For example, the United States Air Force is the Pentagon's designated agent for procuring defense satellites for all the military services.

The above expert advice infers that, through a rigorous systems approach, it is conceivable that a new fleet of air tankers could be developed simultaneously with an upgraded nationwide infrastructure of air tanker bases and command and control centers. This would improve the probability that a new generation of large air tankers would be properly employed for efficient aerial firefighting.

Lead Planes

The Forest Service fleet of twin-engine Beechcraft Baron 58 aircraft is at a critical juncture. Used primarily as lead planes to guide large air tankers during retardant drops, these aircraft are certified for a 10,000-hour structural lifetime. The Forest Service fleet has typically accrued about 6,300 flight hours per aircraft. If limited to a standard Baron climb-cruise-descent profile, the aircraft probably could continue to fly safely for the full 10,000-hour lifetime the manufacturer expects. Some engineering evaluations indicate that the Forest Service Barons can be flown as lead planes for several more thousand hours, but recent problems suggest that the aircraft are nearing the end of their useful, safe firefighting lives and should not be flown in fire support missions much longer.

Last summer, the Baron fleet was only available for lead plane missions about 50% of the time, due to a variety of maintenance problems, according to Forest Service officials. Several emergency landings were recorded in the last few years, as well. Structural concerns surfaced in June, when a Baron 58P landed with wrinkles in its wing skin after experiencing in-flight turbulence. Inspection by a manufacturer's engineer concluded no structural damage had occurred.

Limited test data acquired a number of years ago indicate that these aircraft were not subjected to undue stresses while operating as lead planes, the panel was told. Still, it is clear that Barons are subjected to significant turbulence near fires. NASA studies showed that firefighting aircraft encounter abnormal maneuver and gust loads, and that the loads significantly shorten the structural life of an aircraft. The panel was unable to determine whether the results of an instrumented study were ever used to alter the manufacturer's standard Baron inspection and structural repair cycle.

Accelerated-aging factors have been used in Canada to improve the safety margins of aircraft structures, and are part of Canada's firefighting aircraft airworthiness certification and maintenance process. For example, Canadian government authorities and contractors developed an accelerated-aging factor of up to seven for each hour that an aircraft spends in specified fire-support activities. One firefighting flight hour might be equivalent to seven "normal" flight hours; this significantly shortens inspection and structural maintenance intervals, and ultimately, aircraft life. While Forest Service Barons are used in the firefighting environment, and are subjected to higher-than-normal stresses, there was no indication that any similar accelerated-aging formula is applied to account for time logged over a fire zone.

Absent supporting data, the panel is inclined to believe that the remaining structural life of these Barons is shorter than 3,700 flight hours. Consequently, the long-term sustainability of this fleet, particularly from a structural standpoint, must be considered in doubt. The panel heard that, in the absence of a rigorous engineering analysis backed by flight test data and FAA review, it is not possible to ensure that the aircraft are airworthy to continue operating as firefighting lead planes.

Helicopters

Because most of the fire suppression and support helicopter fleet is FAA-certified and generally operated within the limits of their design while firefighting, the panel has little reason to question the fleet's sustainability. The only concern voiced during presentations was related to ex-military helicopters, which are operated under a Restricted Category type certificate, and must be considered FAA "orphans," similar to the ex-military air tanker situation. The panel is unaware of any other helicopter airworthiness issues that would raise a sustainability question, although operational improvements could enhance safety and efficiencies. The public-use aircraft issue and the accompanying question about FAA oversight exemption also remain (See Finding 6 - Certification).

FINDING 4–MISSION

The variety of missions, philosophies, and unclear standards of federal land management agencies creates a "mission muddle" that seriously compromises the safety and effectiveness of aviation in wildland fire management.

Although a unified command and control arrangement would be ideal to improve the effectiveness of the aerial firefighting task, this is unlikely to occur anytime soon. The panel believes that risks remain higher than necessary because the mission differences among agencies have not been recognized, reconciled, and expressed as a common operations plan with clear lines of authority. The efficiency and safety of air operations could be markedly increased by such a plan, which also could mitigate the perception that resources are not being well used.

Jurisdictions and federal- and state-agency responsibilities must be reconciled to develop a more effective national wildland aerial firefighting program. Many mandates are based on constitutional arrangements, and it will likely be difficult to share duties and delegate or transfer activities. But with the right motivation, such reorganizations are possible. The United States and Canada were motivated by an external threat to develop the North American Aerospace Defense Command, which created an effective binational arrangement, despite command and national sovereignty compromises. Later, largely to maintain global economic strength, the United States also entered into the North American Free Trade Agreement with Canada and Mexico. Some sovereignty was ceded and many processes were revolutionized, but each of the three partner nations is now stronger economically.

The value of forests as a national resource could be considered as important as defense and free trade. Consequently, wildland fire protection should be treated as an element of national security. To that end, the necessity for a more-effective aerial firefighting management process is so compelling that the panel believes removing obstacles to a more effective organizational structure would yield major dividends.

Highly dedicated and experienced land managers involved in aerial firefighting are attempting to reconcile differing missions, while operating with inadequate aviation policies and standards. Both the BLM and Forest Service practice decentralized management of actual wildland fires. However, the fire management program area in the BLM is centralized, while it is decentralized in the Forest Service. This situation fosters ineffectiveness and inefficiency.

The panel is aware of useful, well-intentioned interagency coordination and cooperation arrangements, and these represent commendable efforts by people working in agencies that have juxtaposed or overlapping mandates. The arrangements are valuable for developing compatible policies and standards. However, questions arise as to effectiveness and efficiency of systems that require six or more separate national interagency coordinating bodies to agree on an action to be taken.

Comments on a few points in the Standards for Fire and Aviation Operations 2002 manual illustrate the situation:

- The National Multi-Agency Coordination Group is mandated to establish "priorities and direction for wildland fire activities." Each member of this seven-agency committee, which operates by consensus and is convened only during active fire situations, has a veto. Similar National Multi-Agency Coordination Groups are formed as needed in various geographic areas to deal with regional firefighting issues. Members of the national group offered the view that this process was not cumbersome. However, the panel heard from front-line aerial firefighters that "the feds don't fight fire in the morning because all the leaders are in meetings." It is the panel's belief that a group based on decision making by consensus is an inefficient way to handle the resource allocation challenges of a wildland fire's rapidly changing circumstances or the competing demands of numerous fires.

- The section in Standards for Fire and Aviation Operations 2002, "Forest Service Agency Specific Directions, Aviation Operations," begins with a statement that, "There are numerous differences between Department of Interior and Forest Service Aviation Policy." Many statements throughout the document indicate that individual agencies are "committed to interagency, consistent development and application." However, other statements indicate that it is possible for agencies to depart from the standards or to supplement them with others, underscoring agencies' inconsistency when it comes to cooperation and collaboration.

- The Federal Fire and Aviation Safety Team oversees and monitors "national fire and aviation safety practices" and makes "recommendations to improve safety and prevent accidents." However, the Interagency Incident Team Evaluation begins with questions about accomplishing objectives of the Wildland Fire Situation Analysis. The document continues to address considerations of cost effectiveness; sensitivity to resource limits, environmental concerns, political, and social concerns; professionalism of management; and response to changing conditions before safety is mentioned. While each section of the Standards for Fire and Aviation Operations begins with a strong statement about safety, the Incident Team Evaluation places safety well down the list, which might convey to those being evaluated that safety is not a priority.

Aviation Resource Use

An on-site incident commander directs individual fire suppression efforts, while the National Multi-Agency Coordination Group allocates resources and establishes relationships on a geographic, "big-picture" basis. Although there is a clear and authoritative command structure in place on individual fires, national aerial fire suppression resources are not always safely and effectively deployed.

Through multiple presentations, it was obvious to the panel that there is no clear, general understanding of the degree to which fire detection and initial attack are priorities. The panel was told that the "states want to kill fires and the Forest Service wants to manage them." Many presenters expressed concern about whether a small fire should be attacked aggressively or on-site personnel should "manage it to benefit resource values." The panel was told that an unwritten Forest Service policy was to "let it burn, then try to put it out once it was out of control," an opinion disputed by Forest Service officials. Several people who appeared before the panel stated that lack of aggressive initial attack provided an opportunity for controllable fires to become escaped wildland fires. One presenter stated that fires spread for two reasons, a "let-it-burn" philosophy and the "inability to get resources on the job, often due to rules."

There appeared to be widespread concern that large air tankers were being used to "build line" on large fires and were unavailable to control small fires, thus increasing the probability that small fires would become uncontrollable. Several individuals said that they believed that large air tankers were being used on some large fires only to provide the public with an impression that "something was being done." Some asserted that California, by launching a strong initial attack then scaling back, as appropriate, has a true initial attack policy.

The foregoing is, in the assessment of the panel, a clear indication that the unreconciled missions of various organizations result in a confusing diversity of efforts to suppress wildland fires. One issue presented to the panel with the strongest consensus was that a reduced emphasis on initial attack is harmful to the firefighting mission of land management agencies.

FINDING 5–CULTURE, ORGANIZATIONAL STRUCTURE, AND MANAGEMENT

The culture, organizational structure and management of federal wildland fire management agencies are ill suited to conduct safe and effective aviation operations in the current environment.

There is a strong culture in federal land management agencies derived from an almost obsessive dedication to wildland management, but employees are working with an unclear mission and outdated organizational structures. The panel saw the federal agencies' collective culture as the product of many years of professional attention to forest and other wildland management activities in conjunction with wildlife conservation. As the size and complexity of various agencies grew, so did a requirement to develop the skills and organizational structure needed to manage large organizations. Although each agency's culture was formed in relative isolation, a comfortable working relationship exists among contemporaries today.

Highly technical and professional organizations are usually not as proficient in managerial activities as they are in their professional specialties. In the past, the opinions of experts within each agency established, implemented, and directed programs. Today, many well-financed interest groups generate plausible, although often not scientifically supported, ideas that drive public opinion. The rhetoric of public debate rather than sound science often initiates policy change. Experts within government agencies can no longer assume that their opinions will prevail, even if they are supported by unassailable science.

Through an apparent "what-seems-best-for-us" approach, there have been fundamental divergences in the structure of some firefighting organizations. A decentralized structure suited the Forest Service's initial responsibilities, while the BLM chose a centralized structure. Other federal agencies have organizations that reflect the requirements of their mandated missions.

Today, a coalition of agencies administers the federal aviation and ground firefighting programs. An examination of the joint structure would determine an appropriate balance of centralized and decentralized management. The panel notes that many large organizations operate well with centralized policy, standards, and funding control. Simultaneously, those organizations deliver services through a decentralized operations program that allows initiative and field-level discretion.

The panel is not aware of an efficient arrangement where a decentralized organization (such as the Forest Service) shares operational responsibilities with a highly centralized organization (such as the BLM). The achievement of a goal, such as "we want to work as one at the fires," is within reach, but not with the present mix of interagency management structures and missions.

Culture and Funding

The presentation of land management agencies' requirements and priorities, including the aviation program, to obtain appropriate funding is clouded by agency cultures. This results in appropriations that are based on what the agencies have been able to justify for predicted activities. Large supplementary appropriations, typically triggered when fires grow to a certain size, suggest that the base funding profile is insufficient to control fires, while too much funding is devoted to the control of escaped wildland fires. Escaped fires include those associated with uncontrollable events, such as lightning strikes, semi-controllable events, such as human carelessness, and escaped prescribed burns.

The apparent, but possibly illusory, reality that funding is never sufficient has bred a culture that accommodates risk in aerial firefighting activities. For the aviation program overall, this has translated to insufficient contract funding to provide adequate knowledge of aircraft condition; insufficient training, inspection, and maintenance; and deplorable safety record for large air tankers. Similarly, the government-owned and operated Baron and Sherpa fleets are apparently aging prematurely, and are being dispatched into conditions where they cannot maintain altitude if one engine fails.

A culture that emphasizes cost-efficiency has also created an admirable, but hazardous, "can-do" ethos that pervades firefighting aviation. Unwittingly, the Forest Service has exploited the passion and willingness of its firefighters to do more with less. But this approach fails to confront an incompatibility with safe aviation—considering cost when there is not a clear understanding of the effects that result from apparent savings. A cost emphasis also sends strong signals to operators and supervisors to encourage and reward a "can-do" attitude, despite a shortage of resources or having to compromise safety. As one regional aviation officer commented, "We are captured by our own success; we always manage to find a way."

Firefighters have become almost completely reactive by accepting shortages as a standard way-of-life. This leads pilots and other firefighters to take more shortcuts and risks every season. Shifting from a "can-do" culture based on chronic shortages to practices based on viewing fire emergencies as a "business," where sustainable performance replaces crisis management, would seem to enhance overall air operations safety. Management attention can alter "can-do" attitudes and foster a more effective, safer culture. For example, the panel heard presentations describing operations that yield lower accident rates in California and Canada, where strong safety programs support adequate training and maintenance.

Dedication to the professional aspects of land management has led to a patchwork of interagency committees that respect the mandates of partner organizations, but do not resolve basic aerial firefighting organizational and accountability issues. This has resulted in what was described to the panel as many forestry professionals in technical management positions that govern aviation programs. Regardless of their dedication, it is impossible for these managers to determine the technical requirements for a complex aviation program. This situation has contributed to a deterioration of Forest Service and BLM aviation's overall level of safety, which is exacerbated by the FAA's minimal oversight and weak Restricted Category aircraft certification process (See Finding 6).

Leadership

The panel saw evidence of good leadership that could help to ensure effectiveness, efficiency, and safety in the federal aerial firefighting program. However, differing missions and incompatible organizational structures make any leader's task very difficult. Many federal and contractor employees working on the ground expressed concerns about the leadership of government aviation programs, with respect to safety. It is the function of leaders to ensure that those in the field, whether government or contractor employees, work in safe conditions. The often-repeated acceptance by those in federal service and industry that firefighting "is a risky business" is intolerable. Risks must be analyzed and mitigated, not accepted as part of life. For example, employees should not be flying in aircraft that cannot perform safely in all anticipated conditions. Neither should aircraft be dispatched when there is any doubt about their airworthiness. If leaders, by their conduct, give clear signals that safe operations are paramount, those following will know what to do. Such conduct by managers will minimize the probability that crews will fly aircraft in unsafe environments, and help to ensure proper aircraft maintenance and airworthiness.

It appeared to the panel that Forest Service and BLM leaders were not well versed on aircraft certification, airworthiness, and performance issues, nor their implications for flight safety. The FAA's airworthiness standard insists that the probability of an air carrier aircraft not completing its flight and landing safely due to any airworthiness failure must be less than one in a billion. The panel was unable to determine what should be an acceptable FAA airworthiness standard for large air tankers. However, an acceptable standard is certainly not reflected in airworthiness failures that led to the loss of two large aircraft in this year's 8,000 or so hours flown by that fleet. Neither is it reflected in the total of 8 to 10 structural failures (the cause of some were not clearly identified) associated with former military aircraft employed in aerial firefighting.

There seems to be little justification for a culture that accepts firefighting aircraft airworthiness standards that are less than those required of transport category aircraft. Nor is there justification for firefighting aircraft airworthiness standards to be less than those required of standard-use aircraft. Turbulence and smoke near fires create sufficiently difficult operating conditions without crews having to worry about their aircraft shedding its wings. There is no justifiable reason for national and aviation program leaders to defer decisive action on airworthiness issues.

Leaders also have an obligation to determine and articulate the organization's mission. Unfortunately, collaboration among the many federal and state agencies associated with firefighting, each with a different mission and culture, has created a situation where engaging all employees and contractors in a clearly defined task is difficult. In all organizations, leaders must be relentless in their efforts to develop a reconciled set of tasks for which there is explicit responsibility and accountability. Only then can an organization establish and implement strategies and plans that yield well-defined results. This leads to good decisions about environmental impacts, social issues, employment practices, contracting, and required legislative changes.

It is a generally accepted principle of management that leaders also must develop effective relationships. For Forest Service and BLM managers, these would include direct employees, contract employees, state agencies, and other federal agencies. The panel was told there was "no regular consultation" among these groups. Instead, there were "rules without consultation," and "no input into the contract." Effective relationships will allow employees to function in a clearly understood environment.

Presenters told the panel that, during past budget reallocations, many employees were encouraged to retire early, and certain management positions were eliminated. Although unavoidable at the time, those actions have created a shortage of experienced middle managers. Agency leaders now face a time-critical requirement to ensure that there are enough managers to meet future needs. This will involve significant training and a conscious delegation of authority to the lowest possible level. Development of future top managers could force many old practices to be abandoned, and might lead to issues being resolved on the basis of what is best for federal agencies' aerial firefighting function.

Pilot Culture

In presentations to the panel, it was clear that some managers were aware of crews taking aircraft into areas where they could not return if they lost an engine. Pilots, particularly pilots flying large air tankers, too often accept risks to accomplish a mission. With each passing season, crews discover they can accept a little more risk than before and still survive, and be paid for doing so. Risk becomes addictive, additive, and accepted. Risk is, as some indicated to the panel, one of the most attractive features of the mission. Risk can be mitigated to a degree by what crews learn on the job while fighting fires.

Although few lives might be at risk, large air tankers are being flown in unsafe conditions that the military would not usually accept. Air tanker pilots convey a spirit of invincibility. Presenters' clear admiration for pilots who take unwarranted risks in the name of mission accomplishment was seen too frequently to suggest that this is a deliberate, restrained population. Extensive documentation also indicates that aircraft limits have been consistently exceeded. The 1974 NASA study found g limits were consistently exceeded, and alarming descent speeds were frequently used (See Finding 3 - Aircraft). The Interagency Air tanker Board noted in its December 1987 meeting notes that, "it is a documented fact that the air tankers are regularly operated outside operational limits. Little supervision, standardization, and training, (the antidote to risk), have been developed."

Business-like Operations

California and Canada offer models that land management agencies can examine to see how other government organizations function under established business principles. In an appropriately structured organization, solid management promotes adequate funding for safe, effective aviation programs based on sound business acumen and backed by verifiable research.

The panel heard an often-stated desire that wildland aerial firefighting should be more business-like, but presenters said current practices often fall short of that goal. Being business-like implies numerous attributes, including effectiveness, efficiency, reliability, integrity, and clearly expressed values. There seems to be little in the way of reliable database information to help measure the effectiveness or efficiency in either the Forest Service or the BLM. Although requests by the panel were willingly accepted, information was often not produced, or it was submitted in a form that had limited usefulness in measuring effectiveness or efficiency. Development of data in a form that is useful for these purposes is difficult, particularly in an environment of rapidly changing technology and chronic resource restraint.

The absence of good data to measure performance is common to many organizations. To compound the difficulty, developing effective performance measures for wildland firefighting is a challenge. The panel was offered examples of effective performance measures, such as the cost-per-acre of fire suppression. However, costs are likely to be high on a per-acre basis for small fires, while it is virtually impossible to estimate the dollars saved by quickly extinguishing fires. Efficient data collection and analysis tools are available that could improve the effectiveness of firefighting operations. These would be most effective when accompanied by clarification of missions, assignment of authorities, and revision to organizational structures.

The 25-year-old National Fire Management Analysis System, which is used to estimate cost-benefit considerations and is the best tool currently available, is being revised. However, this model does not consider non-commodity values, such as public concerns, aesthetics, wildlife, or endangered species. From presentations made to the panel, it appears that the model is not well understood. Additionally, the model makes land value distinctions based on averages too broad to be helpful in specific situations.

A significant impediment to Forest Service and BLM aviation operations and other land-management elements is the lack of a common mission statement backed by the authority necessary to achieve that mission. At the moment, there seems to be no clear and well-understood system of command and control, and little clarity in determining what missions and objectives take precedence. To resolve these deficiencies, Forest Service officials said they are working to replace the current crisis-mode approach with a more deliberate strategy, viewing fire not as an emergency but as a part of day-to-day business.

While there were many expressions of a desire to be a single business-like, interagency operation when dealing with wildland fires, numerous contradictions were found. On one hand, there were many claims of aerial firefighting elements being "seamless over the fire" and having "one aviation program." But examples also were given of helicopters not being dispatched to a fire because no Forest Service helicopter manager was available, as required by agency policy, and helicopters being withdrawn from state land when flames spread to federal land because again there were no helicopter managers on-site.

It is unlikely that people will understand why helicopters operating on federal land are subject to different rules than those operating on state land. Nor should people be expected to accept that helicopters might be withdrawn from a fire, simply because it has spread across a jurisdictional boundary. If firefighting agencies want public support, they must accomplish retardant and water drops that meet the expectations of people and their elected representatives or explain why another approach is better. The difficulty of explaining why firefighting helicopters used by one level of government must be grounded by another level of government, while the latter transfers in managers, compromises an agency's credibility.

A principle of business is that, in the process of production and exchange, there must be an advantage to both the producer and the consumer or the business will fail. During wildland fire suppression efforts, there are an increasing number of dwellings that are destroyed. For those who lose their homes, and the millions who view or read about the losses, a perception exists that current firefighting methods provide little advantage to the "consumer," the taxpayer, in this case.

It is unlikely that the consumers would accept an explanation that there is numerous differences between Forest Service and Department of Interior aviation policies, or that the National Multi-Agency Coordination Committee was developing priorities and direction by consensus, while a fire advanced toward a community. Clear mandates, accountabilities, and logical lines of authority are vital to operating an interagency firefighting aviation program in a business-like way.

An element of a business-like operation is treating all concerned with courtesy. The panel found that many employees of the Forest Service and the BLM exhibited a very high degree of courtesy and candor. This is a reflection of good leadership and suggests that if organizational impediments, together with the uncertainty of missions and funding, were eliminated, agencies' leaders could better satisfy taxpayer expectations.

The objective of being business-like is based on a desire to realize levels of operational effectiveness typically found in the commercial business sector. However, operational effectiveness requires sensible, specific measures of factors associated with effectiveness. Without accurate metrics, fire agencies cannot accurately determine the cost, effectiveness, or sustainability of current or proposed firefighting systems.

FINDING 6–CERTIFICATION

The Federal Aviation Administration (FAA) has abrogated any responsibility to ensure the continued airworthiness of "public-use" aircraft, including ex-military aircraft converted to firefighting air tankers. Although these aircraft are awarded FAA type certificates, the associated certification processes do not require testing and inspection to ensure that the aircraft are airworthy to perform their intended missions.

Public-use aircraft are operated to fulfill a government function that meets certain conditions under Title 49 of United States Code 40102(a)(37). They are believed to be unique in the United States aviation sector because they are "generally exempt from complying with Federal Aviation Regulations," according to FAA Advisory Circular AC 00-1.1. When operating in the aerial firefighting role under federal contracts, ex-military aircraft, which constitute a substantial portion of the current large air tanker fleet, are considered public-use aircraft. Typically, public-use aircraft were Air Force and Navy transports and antisubmarine patrol aircraft, built to carry cargo and conduct long-range flights. They were retired from active military service for a variety of reasons and subsequently released to the Forest Service and private operators for conversion to air tankers carrying and delivering fire retardant.

The panel found that Forest Service and BLM leaders do not have a good understanding of the FAA's certification and oversight role regarding public-use aircraft. Additionally, they have placed an unjustifiable faith in the FAA's oversight of ex-military firefighting air tankers. Therefore, Forest Service and BLM personnel, contract operators, and aircrews are in the untenable position of having to determine whether an aircraft is safe to fly. As expected, they are often not qualified or equipped to make that assessment.

The Occupational Safety and Health Administration (OSHA) requires that all United States employees be provided with a safe workplace environment. Private companies must adhere to strict safety standards, but public aircraft operations are allowed to operate under exceptions to OSHA rules and regulations. Operators of public aircraft, including firefighting air tankers, are covered by lower safety standards than any other sector of

United States aviation or public transportation. This exception standard adversely affects the safety of contractor air tanker crews and federal government pilots.

The FAA apparently sees no statutory requirement to ensure the airworthiness of public-use aircraft, particularly air tankers. This position has led to a dangerous misunderstanding throughout the aerial firefighting community. Under federal law, the FAA is responsible for ensuring that former military aircraft are approved for specialized operations, including firefighting. Once modified to an air tanker configuration, both civil and ex-military aircraft operate under a Restricted Category type certificate, which limits how they can be flown in the firefighting mission. The current fleet of aircraft, such as the C-130A, P-2V, P-3 and other military types, has been awarded type certificates under FAR 21.25(a)(2). This regulation states that an aircraft "has been manufactured and accepted for use by the United States military, and later modified for a special purpose," and "no feature or characteristic . . . makes it unsafe when operated under limitations prescribed for its intended use," according to an FAA briefing to the panel. An associated regulation, FAR 21.25(b), restricts aircraft operation to special purposes, such as firefighting.

FAA Roles

FAA regulations, and the type certificates awarded under them, do not ensure that the FAA has determined that aircraft are airworthy or suitable for safe, long-term operation in a demanding aerial firefighting environment. They only require a potential operator to advise regional FAA officials that the aircraft was designed and built for a military mission, and that the aircraft is not unsafe when operated in the firefighting role. A Restricted Category type certificate governs how the aircraft is operated, and a Supplemental type certificate approves conversion modifications related to the firefighting mission, such as retardant tank installations. A Data Sheet accompanying the type certificate and Supplemental type certificate stipulates what records, manuals, military documents, and instructions for continued airworthiness must accompany the aircraft, according to the FAA presentation to the panel.

Civil aircraft converted to air tankers, but previously operated in passenger or cargo roles, such as Douglas DC-6s, were originally required to undergo a rigorous airworthiness certification process, including instrumented flight-testing. However, these aircraft have inspection and maintenance programs designed for air transport operations, not firefighting, where turbulence and aggressive low-level maneuvering stress the aircraft. Although the two environments are sufficiently different to warrant air tankers having modified maintenance programs tailored to firefighting, there is no government requirement for one, the panel was told.

The FAA's Restricted Category certification and continued airworthiness process also does not require the aircraft's Original Equipment Manufacturer to have any interaction with the current operator. This is a subtle but important point concerning ongoing maintenance and airworthiness assurance of ex-military aircraft converted to air tankers. The Original Equipment Manufacturer might not be aware that a third party, an air tanker operator, for example, has been awarded a civil type certificate for a former military aircraft. Further, all ex-military aircraft historical records might be retained by the

Department of Defense, not the manufacturer. In the case of Lockheed-built C-130As, the Department of Defense possesses the records and engineering data package, a fact that has hampered civilian operators of the A-model Hercules. Without engineering data and historical records, it is difficult to determine what inspections should be conducted and at what intervals. The situation also complicates development of maintenance and structural repair programs needed to ensure that an aircraft flying firefighting missions can be operated safely for an extended lifetime.

Once an ex-military aircraft enters service as an air tanker under contract to the Forest Service or other federal agency, it falls into a "gray area" in terms of airworthiness assurance processes. The aircraft is then operated in a public aircraft or public-use category. According to the FAA, flying under Public Aircraft Operations, as defined in 49 U.S. Code 40125, is "not dependent solely on [aircraft] airworthiness status or certification." When performing a mission for the federal government, the aircraft is considered a public-use vehicle and is exempt from most FAA oversight and most federal regulations governing civil aircraft.

Essentially, when an aircraft becomes a public-use vehicle, the FAA ignores its airworthiness status. Operators are on their own to define inspection and maintenance programs that ensure airworthiness. FAA inspectors check air tanker operators' records to verify that operations are being conducted in accordance with regulations, but rarely, if ever, physically inspect an aircraft to ensure that it is safe to fly an intended mission. Consequently, public-use aircraft have a history of accidents because they operate under a federally sanctioned double standard—airworthiness and safety measures required of private operators, such as airlines and air charter companies, do not apply to government aircraft operations. Although this issue extends well beyond aerial firefighting, it must be considered when trying to create a safe environment for this community, and it is a critical factor that cannot be resolved without strong FAA leadership and interagency cooperation.

Airworthiness Orphans

Today's convoluted FAA Restricted Category and public-use certification situation has led to ex-military aircraft, particularly large air tankers and former military helicopters, being adrift and isolated in an airworthiness sense. Large air tankers, in particular, are airworthiness "orphans," relegated to a low FAA priority. The fleet is small, and the FAA is not staffed or trained to deal with unusual airworthiness issues that characterize 40 to 50-year-old aircraft, especially ex-military air tankers that were never subjected to a rigorous FAR Part 23 or Part 25 certification process.

Based on discussions between the panel and Forest Service leaders, it is clear that the agency has a poor understanding of the FAA's air tanker airworthiness certification process and its limitations. Agency officials have long believed that any ex-military aircraft certified by the FAA essentially was guaranteed to be airworthy and capable of safely performing the contract-required firefighting mission. That is not the case, as confirmed by senior FAA representatives.

The FAA's lack of airworthiness-related support for Restricted Category and public-use aircraft extends to the inspection and maintenance areas, forcing the Forest Service to assume the untenable position of being both a contracting agency and regulator. In trying to do both, it does neither well. The agency cannot require its aircraft contractors to ensure a high-level of safety and quality maintenance, yet provide the associated necessary oversight, while also striving to obtain the lowest-price services possible (See Finding 7 - Contracting). The Forest Service has neither the skilled technical staff nor the budgets to ensure air tanker airworthiness. That, it believes, is the FAA's responsibility. But the FAA is not doing that job, leaving the responsibility to aircraft operators, who are encouraged by the Forest Service contracting process to minimize maintenance costs. Consequently, cooperation and good working relationships have become expensive casualties of Forest Service and air tanker operator interactions. This unsafe situation will persist unless the system switches to new contracting processes backed by active FAA oversight and participation.

Canada's Approach

Canada also certifies its firefighting air tankers in the Restricted Category, but goes well beyond FAA criteria. Transport Canada (the nation's aircraft certification body) adds Special Conditions to cover Special Purpose Operations as part of its large aircraft certification in the Restricted Category. A Canadian Airworthiness Manual Advisory requires operators to develop plans for "the structure to resist and/or tolerate fatigue damage in the environment peculiar to the special-purpose role." The manual requires consideration of any available information related to that aircraft's fatigue life limitations, such as the ability of principal structural elements to tolerate damage.

As an example of how Canadian operators comply with these requirements, Conair Aviation Ltd. developed a Supplemental Structural Inspection Document for its Fokker F-27 Firefighter aircraft, and then submitted it to Transport Canada's Continuing Airworthiness Aircraft Certification Branch chief for approval. This document adjusts the F-27's standard structural inspection time intervals and limitations "to account for the increased severity of the time spent in the firefighting role [as] compared to typical Fokker F-27 transport role operation," according to the Conair plan. The company has developed a set of formulas to calculate the degree that an aircraft's lifetime is reduced when flying the fire retardant-delivery portion of an air tanker mission. In essence, multiplication of retardant-delivery flight time by a damage-rate factor accelerates the aging of certain structural elements. This process acknowledges that the time spent in the firefighting role imposes more severe loads on the aircraft, perhaps 5 to 10 times greater than what it would experience in a typical passenger-transport role, and accounts for the increased loads by shortening the intervals between inspections.

Canada's certification process encourages cooperation between regulators and private operators. Transport Canada officials work closely with operators in developing Supplemental Structural Inspection Documents ensuring that the right expertise is involved in developing a quality inspection program to provide pilots with structurally sound aircraft. From a business perspective, the operator can better predict how long the aircraft can be operated safely, and can then develop a suitable replacement plan.

In the United States, air tanker operators, with sufficient financial resources and engineering expertise, might elect to inspect and repair their aircraft more frequently than required under military or civil transport maintenance plans to protect their investments and ensure flight crew safety. But there is no FAA requirement to do so, little or no FAA assistance or oversight, and the Forest Service does not contractually reward such extra measures. As a result, the more safety-conscientious operators might sacrifice profit margins, at least in the short term, and risk being priced-out of a Forest Service contract by providing a higher level of safety than the government requires.

FINDING 7–CONTRACTS

Government contracts for air tanker and helicopter fire management services do not adequately recognize business and operational realities or aircraft limitations. As a result, contract provisions contain disincentives to flight safety.

Federal agencies responsible for wildland aerial firefighting have adopted a widespread, short-term pursuit of cost-efficiency. This is an appropriate objective for food contracts, facility upgrades, or buying office supplies. However, when extended to the aviation program, the result might be an undesirable reduction in safety margins, unless the consequences of spending reductions are clearly understood. A narrow cost-focus is evident in Forest Service and BLM contracts that do not reward value, performance, or safety. A lack of clear understanding about the long-term or life-cycle costs is evident in day-to-day fire-management decisions, safety-sensitive positions that remain vacant for extended periods, and asset-related decisions to save money.

While cost-saving is an essential contracting criterion, it appears to have displaced other, less-quantifiable criteria that call for more judgment and experience, such as value, safety records, and past performance. Pilots have sarcastically referred to this cost-focus philosophy as "budget protection" rather than "fire protection." In contrast, a Canadian philosophy states, "We can't spend too much the first day [of a fire]," seems to justify spending money on early containment of a fire, and doing so in an operationally effective way that minimizes the number of escaped fires. In the long run, the Canadians believe that they spend far less for a quick-response capability designed to contain small fires than they do to fight fires after they grow large.

Scarcity Mindset

The aviation problems faced by this nation's wildland firefighting agencies stem from a decades-long scarcity mentality—doing the best job possible with whatever financial resources are available. A well-developed budget justification process used successfully by other government agencies is missing from Forest Service and BLM contracting. Consequently, air tanker operators are encouraged to minimize maintenance, training, and other costs to live within the contracting organizations' budget requirements.

Contracts between the Forest Service and large air tanker operators explicitly neither recognize nor reconcile the differences in missions and expertise among the many government organizations involved in wildland firefighting. For example, technical advice to the Forest Service contracting unit appears to be insufficient. A senior fixed-wing advisor to the contracting service position has been vacant for approximately a year, apparently for budget reasons. For highly technical contracts, such as the provision of firefighting aircraft, the ready availability of expert aviation advice is important to both safety and the price of the purchased services.

Airworthiness Factors

The 2002 National Air tanker Service Contract requires adherence to federal regulations but does not require operators to conduct safe operations. Nothing in the contract requires contractors to operate their aircraft in accordance with maintenance and inspection schedules tailored to the known conditions of an aerial firefighting environment. Studies by NASA and others show that firefighting ages aircraft quicker than the operations for which they were originally designed, such as transporting cargo or flying patrol missions over oceans. The panel was told "aircraft never forget how they have been used," but contract provisions do not account for that reality.

Another situation related to aviation technical expertise that is available to contracting officers is the lack of feedback about air tanker structural problems. The panel saw no evidence that contracting offices either knew about or had attempted to address known structural issues to ensure that contractor aircraft could be operated safely. It is unclear whether contracting offices fully understood the ramifications of what other segments of the firefighting community had discovered or were aware of structural-life concerns.

Several outside studies, such as the 1974 NASA study of DC-6s used in firefighting, highlighted how air tankers were being flown and the resulting impact on aircraft structural life. In addition, the Interagency Air Tanker Board has known for more than 20 years about conditions that led to the in-flight break-up of three C-119 air tankers and the structural failure of a fourth aircraft. The minutes of their 1981, 1987, and 1988 meetings note that the aircraft were exceeding operational limits. The December 1987 meeting noted that, "All air tankers are periodically operated outside their specified limits, but, other than the C-119, their operating history to date indicates they can withstand these excursions without in-flight breakups." The board was inappropriately making airworthiness judgments that were better left to FAA structures engineers. Nevertheless, its findings might not have been relayed clearly to the contracting office, which might have taken positive measures to address air tanker structural problems and enhance aircrew safety.

The panel found nothing in the current air tanker contract that provided incentives for contractors to operate safely. Instead, contracts appear to rely on the FAA's Restricted Certificate of Airworthiness, which declares that an aircraft is "appropriate for use," and does little more than require that it be maintained in accordance with previous military criteria (See Finding 6 - Certification).

Financial penalties assessed for periods when the aircraft are unavailable for service encourage contractors to fly aircraft that are not airworthy. If requirements built into the contract ensured proper maintenance for the mission being flown, a penalty for unavailable aircraft would be reasonable. But contract pricing considerations that do not recognize the special maintenance requirements of firefighting operations, exacerbated by limited FAA oversight, have contributed to losing an average of one large air tanker of an approximately 40-aircraft fleet each fire season.

Cost of Accidents versus Investing in Safety

The Forest Service contracting office told the panel that every term in the large air tanker contract was developed in response to an accident. The expression used was, the "contracts are written in blood." The panel understands that contracts, as presently developed, are heavily influenced by the availability of budgeted funds and do not necessarily consider technical and safety factors adequately. Still, the government's constitutional obligation to provide for people's safety should not be frustrated by unclear lines of responsibility or the lack of resources.

After two large air tankers and crews were lost due to in-flight wing separations during the 2002 fire season, the remaining C-130As and PB4Ys, approximately one quarter of the air tanker fleet, were grounded by the Forest Service and were unavailable for use in a year of unusually heavy firefighting requirements. The contractors continued to receive availability pay for those aircraft, which were considered unsafe to fly. Would it have been more cost-effective to spend the money necessary to proactively inspect and repair these aircraft types, using techniques tailored to the firefighting environment, thus avoiding two tragic accidents and having a quarter of the tanker fleet grounded?

At least one operator has installed a traffic collision-avoidance system in its tankers, and another contractor has proposed installing the system if the contracting authority would contribute to its cost. These safety systems are required and widely used throughout much of today's civil aircraft fleet. The panel is aware that the Forest Service will require a traffic collision-avoidance system in air tankers for the 2003 fire season, substantially reducing the chances of mid-air collisions in the vicinity of a fire or busy airports. However, the agency does not require air tankers to carry cockpit voice or flight data recorders, which have proven extremely valuable to investigators in determining the causes of accidents. With a long-standing, abysmal large air tanker accident rate, the absence of any requirement for either cockpit voice or flight data recorders defies understanding. The panel also does not understand the absence of a contracting requirement to monitor environmental forces during firefighting missions by installing devices, such as recording accelerometers and strain gauges, on at least a sampling of air tankers.

Contractors and federal employees consistently told the panel that aircraft operators are forced to bid prices that are insufficient for adequate training and maintenance. There was also note made of foreign jurisdictions that offer contracts of up to 10 years and 30% higher contract rates than those in the United States to ensure proper training, maintenance, and eventual aircraft replacement. Countries that "would pay better than the United States" included Australia, Canada, and Italy, according to one contractor.

Future Contracts

It appears that appropriately funded contracts with long time frames would foster stability in the aerial firefighting industry and allow contractors to finance replacement aircraft more easily. Currently, Forest Service and BLM contracts are not structured to encourage proposal submissions from new and innovative operators, a situation that tends to accept the status quo.

The panel believes that the key to future improvements in safety, efficiency, and effectiveness of wildland aerial firefighting lies with the contracting process. However, its members also recognize that funding realities can severely limit options available to the Forest Service and BLM aviation programs. To ensure safe, effective operations within funding constraints, the panel was asked to provide strategic guidance to these agencies. Potential contracting alternatives that might be explored include:

- A government-owned/contractor-operated fleet of air tankers. The California Department of Forestry and Fire Protection uses such a system successfully, which might also be applicable to federal aerial firefighting. Crafting a plan that ensures a safe, dependable operation during high-activity fire seasons would probably involve all major stakeholders, from Forest Service and BLM officials to air tanker operators and pilots.

- Delegating more of the wildland aerial firefighting responsibility to the United States military services. The Air National Guard and Air Force/Army Reserve now have fixed- and rotor-wing aircraft equipped for firefighting, which augments the civilian contractor fleet on an as-needed basis. If appropriately equipped, the military could provide additional retardant- and water-delivery services.

- Outsourcing the federal aerial firefighting mission to a private systems contractor. Well-structured financial incentives specified in carefully written government contracts might save taxpayers wildland aerial firefighting costs, while improving results. A number of precedents for outsourcing government activities were recently underscored by the Army's announced intention to outsource almost 214,000 uniformed military and civilian employee positions.

- Another government agency could assume responsibility for the aerial firefighting service. This alternative would allow land management agencies to focus on their primary statutory missions.

FINDING 8–TRAINING

Training is under funded and inadequately specified for helicopters, large air tankers, and other fixed-wing operations.

Since 1975, aerial firefighting accident rates have improved, but, unlike other aviation communities, rates have leveled off at an unacceptably high point. In the panel's view, an absence of training tailored to this community contributes to the stagnant accident rate.

Presentations showed that, in general, aircrews of contract aircraft lack training in contemporary aviation management subjects, such as risk management and crew resource management. The Forest Service has not identified aircrew training requirements, the contract award process does not consider aircrew training accomplishments, nor are training records required as proof of accomplishment. There were no contract incentives found that would encourage operators to retain full time safety officers to supervise and manage aircrew training.

The Forest Service and BLM aviation safety programs do not use benchmarking as a management tool to learn from other training programs. Internet-based training and idea-exchange mechanisms, which are key components of other professional training systems, are not well used by this community.

Aerial firefighters currently do not have an opportunity to fly together in a training environment. In particular, joint, integrated training of large air tanker and other fixed-wing crews is inadequate. Too often, the panel was informed, the first fire of the season is the first flight for some air tanker pilots, and the first integrated firefight for all pilots in the area. Further, each element of the operation knows little about the others, except for what is learned during real-world operations.

The panel was informed that current training does not develop civil firefighting capabilities, such as consistent drop accuracies backed by measures of operational effectiveness. Previous-season data are not used for sustainable, long-term improvements, either. In the view of the panel, these missed training opportunities compromise an opportunity to emphasize that firefighting is teamwork.

Integrated Training

A Canadian operator, Conair, brings tanker pilots, "bird-dog" aircraft crews, air attack officers, and ground crews together for integrated training and, during the fire season, ongoing operational assessments. The Forest Service does not bring fixed-wing, large air tankers, single-engine air tankers, and state assets together, where standards could be established, teamwork enhanced, and communication improved.

Neither, the panel was told, are military units involved in integrated training with civil aerial firefighting crews. For combat purposes, the military services have learned to practice as an integrated aviation team and have established operational exercises that feature a wide range of air assets flying on instrumented ranges where missions are closely monitored, crews trained, systems evaluated, and procedures tested.

The panel was briefed on Forest Service training and safety initiatives being developed by the National Interagency Fire Center that show definite promise. But in times of budget restraint, managers will need determination to protect the training dollars necessary to improve safety records.

Information and Data

Currently, there is insufficient information about the performance limits of various firefighting aircraft to define an effective training program. Good training programs are founded on well-defined missions, such as firefighting, and, in this case, the aerial elements of that mission. Training efforts are most effective when tasks and priorities are agreed to and clearly specified. Once these become clear, it is possible to conduct a requirements analysis, which can then be compared to a competency assessment to form a basis for a rationally determined training program. Programs and courses can then be developed to address the deficiencies.

Various Forest Service studies have referred to instrumented aircraft exceeding operational and structural limits. Until these limits are clearly understood for each type of aircraft employed in firefighting, it will be difficult to either develop attack profiles that respect those limits or train pilots to fly the profiles. The FAA might decide to mandate specific training for large air tanker pilots. If it does not, the Forest Service might be forced, through its contracting process, to specify required training and provide oversight to ensure that training is being conducted.

Large Air Tanker Crews

There is little likelihood, in the view of the panel, that any training program involving large air tankers can be successful without pilot involvement and support. But a number of issues will have to be resolved with this community before initiating a successful large air tanker crew training program.

To understand the training needs of contractor aircrews, it is important to identify some characteristics of the large air tanker-pilot community. From presentations to the panel, it was apparent that pilots are highly experienced, confident, hard-working, exceptionally mission driven, and passionate about their aircraft and capabilities. They conveyed to the panel that they rely on individual skills to beat the odds of being involved in an accident. Yet, the community appears isolated and risk embracing when conducting actual aerial firefighting operations. The crews are insulated from new ideas, shielded from involvement with other fixed-wing crews, and hampered by a lack of nationwide effectiveness measures. Tanker pilots are not on any agency's mailing list for operational or safety communication, they said.

Pilots presented themselves as distrustful of both their own management and that of federal agencies. They reported experiencing "silent intimidation," being subtly expected to not report maintenance or training violations. They felt the absence of an employment "safety net," and asserted that they have no recourse or appeal process if they are fired. Further, many do not seem to feel that the FAA is capable of regulating this industry, leaving each pilot determine aircraft and mission safety. Pilots of large air tankers also conveyed an anxiety about the loss of their mission to military units, to helicopters, and to single-engine air tankers.

Communications

The panel saw that, quite unlike most professional aviation communities, air tanker pilots do not share information about successful techniques, good or bad results, and difficulties encountered during operations. Information exchange among firefighting aviators is essential to improve training and safety, while feedback from pilots would make overall firefighting operations more effective.

Federal firefighting pilot isolation, and an associated high accident rate, contrasts with operations in Canada and California, where lead plane pilots, fire officials, and tanker pilots brief, fly, and debrief as a team. Despite the presence of federal fire supervisors flying above most fires, few records are kept that could improve air operations. There is little post-mission discussion between airborne fire supervisors and air tanker pilots, and little supervisor training about how to evaluate retardant drops.

The panel also heard that, not only is little feedback given to large air tanker pilots, little is sought. Additionally, federal training and operations committees do not obtain information from tanker pilots. No region or agency seeks feedback from or involves tanker pilots in any safety programs, in developing new procedures, or in communicating their observations to the agencies. An exception is the "annual one-week academy," a pilot said, referring to the training that some pilots receive at the National Aerial Firefighting Academy in Arizona. One air tanker pilot was involved in a review of the 1994 crash of Tanker 82, but the panel was advised that no pilots have been involved in accident or operational reviews since then.

From presentations to the panel, it appears that National Guard units carrying Modular Aerial Fire Fighting Systems on C-130s accomplish a lot of training, but little is done with commercial air tanker operators. One result is a gap in understanding about the capabilities and limitations of Modular Aerial Fire Fighting Systems, which might be resolved through better communication and joint training.

The tanker pilot community is a valuable resource for information on topics such as off-season training, lead plane communications, and dispatcher training. This group is rich in capability and opinions, and is eager to share its knowledge and experience. The panel was encouraged to note that a strategic goal of the Forest Service's Aviation Strategic Plan is better contractor training via outreach. Individual pilots appearing before the panel indicated that, at times, training is recorded without actually being accomplished. They offered demands of the job and a shortage of training funds as reasons why this occurs. In the more adequately-funded firefighting operations of California and Canada, there appears to be significantly more training actually completed, thanks to their larger size, which makes internal training more practicable. Additionally, pilots in those jurisdictions are unionized, although no link was made between unionization and training or safety.

Training Topics

The panel received comments that effective training should address subjects of interest to all firefighting pilot communities and achieve some economies-of-scale through joint sessions. Topics mentioned include crew stress and fatigue, turbine engine operations, reporting processes, and workload management.

In other flying communities, Crew Resource Management (working effectively as a crew) has been successfully used to overcome maverick or rogue tendencies as well as the "captain is boss, don't question him" attitude. This is an important area of interest for the firefighting community, because most new pilots come from single-seat or light aircraft backgrounds and are unaccustomed to operating as part of a crew. If extended to other elements of firefighting air operations, this type of training might mitigate concerns that the panel heard about simplified procedures for frequency use during firefighting operations, standardizing radio calls about distances from the fire, and establishing firefighting standards, such as flight patterns.

The panel was encouraged to hear that the Forest Service and BLM are progressing toward integrated training and focusing on stated topics of interest. In February 2003, the Forest Service's Rocky Mountain Region 2 will hold an air operations training session in Grand Junction, CO. The objective of the training session is to extend crew resource management principles beyond flight-deck basics, adding impetus to broader teamwork by involving more than just the flight crews. The February session will include ground crews, dispatchers, and others involved in fighting fire. The region's initiative also provides an opportunity to overcome difficulties in training with air attack and Air Tactical Group Supervisors, a group that experiences chronic personnel shortages.

Helicopter Training

Helicopter operations are similarly isolated from other air activities, and, from what the panel was told, the crews learn little about the other elements of aerial firefighting, even when everyone is working over a wildland fire. For example, helicopter pilots might receive instructions to maintain a certain distance from a fire while fixed-wing tankers make their drops. Consequently, except by chance, helicopter aircrews do not know or learn much about fixed-wing tanker capabilities and limitations.

Helicopter accident records show numerous examples of handling problems, such as attempting to hover outside the flight envelope, becoming entangled with their own external loads, and wire strikes. They point to deficiencies in training that could minimize such generally avoidable accidents. Similarly, helicopter mechanical failure rates raise the question of adequate funding for maintenance and training of helicopter mechanics.

Appendix A—Members of Blue Ribbon Panel on Aerial Wildland Firefighting

James E. Hall (co-chair)

Jim Hall is a leading expert on transportation safety and security, crisis management and government relations. He has served government and private clients for more than 35 years.

Hall has been counsel to the Senate Subcommittee on Intergovernmental Relations and a member of the staff of U.S. Senator Al Gore, Sr. He joined the administration of Tennessee Governor Ned McWherther as a member of the governor's cabinet and served as director of the state's Planning Office for five years. He returned to Washington, D.C. to serve as chief of staff for Senator Harlan Mathews. President Clinton nominated Hall to serve as a member of the National Transportation Safety Board in 1993, and he was named NTSB chairman from 1994 to 2001.

As NTSB chair, Hall oversaw a period of unprecedented activity as the NTSB investigated numerous major aviation, rail, pipeline and maritime accidents in the U.S. and assisted in many international accident investigations. Under his leadership, the safety board issued landmark safety studies on commuter airlines, the air tour industry, the performance and use of child restraint systems, the dangers to children from passenger-side airbags in automobiles, personal watercraft, transit bus operations, and railway passive grade crossings. In 1996, President Clinton named Hall to the White House Commission on Aviation Safety and Security. Hall is currently serving on the National Academy of Engineering's Committee on Combating Terrorism and the Aviation Institute Advisory Board of George Washington University.

James B. Hull (co-chair)

Jim Hull is the State Forester and Director of the Texas Forest Service in College Station, Texas. He is a 36-year veteran of the Texas Forest Service, having graduated from the School of Forestry at Stephen F. Austin State University in Nacogdoches, Texas. He has extensive experience in all areas of forestry, especially forest management, policy, wildfire protection and administration. In 1996, Hull was selected by The Texas A&M Board of Regents to become the 7th State Forester of Texas. As Director of Texas Forest Service, Hull was responsible for all matters pertaining to forestry in Texas.

Hull provides leadership on numerous forestry boards and organizations at the state, regional, and national level. He serves as chair of the Fire Protection Committee of National Association of State Foresters and as the NASF representative on the National Wildland Fire Leadership Council. He was elected as a Fellow in the Society of American Foresters in 1988 and has received many other prestigious honors and awards throughout his career.

Ken Johnson

Ken Johnson received a Bachelor of Commerce degree from the University of British Columbia and later qualified as a Certified General Accountant. He qualified as a pilot in the Royal Canadian Air Force and gained advanced flying experience as a civilian pilot and in the Air Force reserve, which included arctic surveillance, transport, search and rescue, and fighter duties. In 1967, Johnson joined the Department of Transport as a civil aviation inspector. In 1972, he became the planning manager for the Department's Central Region in Winnipeg. Following an assignment as a policy advisor with the Arctic Transportation Agency, Johnson became the Regional Manager, Airports, Pacific Region, where he was responsible for the operation and development of 25 airports, including Vancouver International. In 1978, he became Director of Airport Policy, Planning /Programming at headquarters in Ottawa.

In 1982, Johnson became the Director of the Department's Aviation Safety Bureau. In 1984, he was appointed Executive Director of the new, independent Canadian Aviation Safety Board. He led that organization as its senior public servant and contributed to the conceptual planning for a multi-modal safety board to encompass the air, marine, rail, and pipeline modes of transport. In 1990, Johnson was appointed Executive Director of the newly established Transportation Safety Board of Canada. He was the TSB's chief operating officer as it developed national and international capabilities in safety investigation until his retirement from the public service in 2001. He has an airline transport pilot's licence and is a member of the Chartered Institute of Transport.

Earl H. McKinney Jr.

Earl McKinney of Bowling Green, Ohio, is an Assistant Professor in the Business School at Bowling Green State University. Before assuming that position, he served in the United States Air Force. His military career included 2,500 hours of flying time as an aircraft commander and instructor pilot in T-37, T-38, F-4, and TG-7 aircraft. He also attended Air Force Safety School and served as a Wing Flying Safety Officer. McKinney has an undergraduate degree from the Air Force Academy, a Master's of Engineering from Cornell University, and a Ph.D. from the University of Texas. McKinney served on the faculty of the Air Force Academy for 9 years.

McKinney has published many articles on aviation safety. He has examined the role of flying experience on crisis decision making, the impact of the familiarity of pilots on crew performance, and the role of communication on early flightdeck team development. He received a grant to study flightdeck communication and performance from the Air Force Air Mobility Command, riding with crews flying refueling missions during Red Flag exercises at Nellis Nevada. McKinney continues to fly, holding a commercial license. He has consulted on a number of aviation projects and has worked on extending Crew Resource Management training to ground controllers for a major carrier. McKinney also contributed to a multiyear Air Force study that considered employment options for new technologies such as Uninhabited Air Vehicles.

William B. Scott

Bill Scott is the Rocky Mountain Bureau Chief for Aviation Week & Space Technology magazine, based in Colorado Springs, CO. In 18 years with Aviation Week, he also has served as Senior National Editor in Washington and in Avionics and Senior Engineering Editor positions in Los Angeles. Focusing primarily on advanced aerospace technology, business, flight testing and military operations, Scott has written more than 2,500 stories for the magazine, and has received 10 editorial awards.

Scott is a Flight Test Engineer graduate of the U.S. Air Force Test Pilot School and a licensed commercial pilot with instrument and multiengine ratings. In 12 years of military and civilian flight testing, in addition to evaluating aircraft for Aviation Week, Scott has logged approximately 2,000 flight hours on 53 types of aircraft. Scott holds a bachelor's in Electrical Engineering from California State University-Sacramento.

Appendix B—Charter for Blue Ribbon Fact Finding Panel on Aviation

The Chief, USDA Forest Service and the Director, Bureau of Land Managment jointly commission this Blue Ribbon Fact Finding Panel on Aviation to identify key information for planning the safe and effective future of the aviation program.

The commission is to determine the adequacy of the current system by identifying weaknesses and failpoints, and to provide information in the following five areas:
- Safety
- Operational effectiveness
- Costs
- Sustainability
- Strategic guidance

It is anticipated that the panel will take an integrated approach to assessing the aviation program. However, at a minimum the panel should address the above topics as they relate to operation and supervision of:
- Airtankers (heavy, medium and single engine airtankers)
- Leadplanes and Air Supervision Modules
- Helicopters
- Air Attack platforms

Panel Members

Jim Hall, (co-chair) Former Chairman, National Transportation Safety Board
Jim Hull, (co-chair) State Forester, Texas
Ken Johnson, Former Executive Director, Transportation Safety Board (Canada)
Earl McKinney, Ph.D., Associate Professor, Bowling Green State University
Bill Scott, Rocky Mountain Bureau Chief, Aviation Week and Space Technology

Dale N. Bosworth   Kathleen Clarke
Chief, USDA Forest Service   Director, Bureau of Land Management

Appendix C—Selected Panel Presentations and Communications[1]

Aerial Firefighting Industry Association. William Broadwell, Executive Director. Statement.

AeroUnion. Chico, CA. Corporate Briefing.

Air Tractor. Olny, TX. Letter and Corporate Briefing.

American Aerostructures. Colorado Springs, CO. Aircraft Platforms. Briefing.

Bombardier Aerospace. Montreal, Canada. Corporate Materials.

Browne, Thomas. Statement.

Buzz Schaffer. E-Mail Letter.

Darran, Walt. E-Mail Letter.

Dave Doan. State of Washington, Department of Natural Resources.

Dominquez, Hank. USDA Fonrest Service, Region 4.

DynCorp Technical Services. Reston, VA. Corporate Briefing.

Erickson Air-Crane, Central Point, OR. Corporate Briefing.

Evergreen Helicopters, McMinnville, OR. Insurance Costs Issues. Briefing Paper.

Gibson, Mark. Timberland Logging. Ashland, Oregon. Letter.

Graves, Marshall. Thoughts on Aerial Firefighting.

Hawkins and Powers. Greybull, WY. Contract Materials and CRM Training Materials.

Herlik, Ed (consultant). Next Generation Air Tankers and correspondence on DOD Issues. Briefing.

Hirth, Connie. Hirth Air Tankers. Buffalo, Wyoming. Statement.

HPTI-Human Performance Training Institute. Englewood, CO. Aviation Safety Issues. Briefing.

International Air Response. Chandler, AZ. CEO Statement and Corporate Documents.

International Institute for Aviation, Science, and Technology. October 2002.

Kelly, Patrick. Retired, Assistant Director, Aviation, USDA Forest Service.

Koenig, Gordon, Statement.

Lehman, William (consultant). Combined Air-Ground Attack on Forest Fires. Briefing

---

[1]A complete list of all organizations and individuals who participated in regional town and government meetings or submitted written information or statements is available at <www.nifc.gov>. Transcripts of the regional town meetings are also available at this website.

LGI. Atlanta, GA. Be-2002. Briefing.

McConnell, John R. (consultant). Scottsdale, AZ. The Ecology of Fires. Briefing.

Meyer, Ron. BLM, Colorado State Office.

Neptune Aviation Services, Missoula, MT. Corporate Presentation.

O'Neil, Sonny. USDA Forest Service, Forest Supervisor, Region 6.

Parker, J.T. E-Mail Letter.

Pyronautics Inc. (J. Biggers, consultant). Prescott AZ. The Phoenix. Briefing.

Rogers Helicopters. Clovis, CA. Helitankers. Corporate Briefing.

Temeku Technologies. New Mexico. The A-10 Firehog. Briefing and CD.

Tierney, Patrick. USDA Forest Service, Region 5.

Watt, John. USDA Forest Service, Region 5.

Wofford, R.L. E-Mail Letter.

Appendix D—References

A Report to the President In Response to the Wildfires of 2000.

Aerial Firefighting Industry Association. October 22, 2002. Letter to Chief of the Forest Service with Attachment; Overview of Aerial Firefighting Industry Association; and National Aerial Firefighting Academy Proposal.

Alderma, K. 1987. *Beech Baron 58P Fatigue Life Program (1980-87)*. Forest Service, Aviation Technology Office.

C-130 Service Life Analysis. 1977.

California Department of Forestry and Fire Protection. March 1994. *Air Operations Program Review*.

California Department of Forestry and Fire Protection. October 2002. Internal Briefing Paper.

ConAir. November 1996. Supplemental Structural Inspection Document.

Department of Agriculture Organic Act of 1944.

Department of the Army. March 1994. Aircrew Training Manual Observation Helicopter.

DOT Federal Aviation Administration. April 19, 1995. Advisory Circular. Government Aircraft Operations.

DOT Federal Aviation Administration. September 26, 2002. Airworthiness Directives: Lockheed C-130 Airplanes.

Economy Acts 1920; Amendments 1932, Section 702–Public Aircraft; Amendments 1994.

FAA Office of Accident Investigations. September 2002. Firefighting Accidents. Accident Investigations Summaries 1984-2002.

Failure Analysis Associates. 1981. *Analysis of Failed Main Landing Gear*.

Fire Suppression Research Report. 1990. *Operational Retardant Evaluation (ORE) Study Status Report*. Intermountain Research Station, RWU-4402. Unpublished report on file at the USDA Forest Service, Washington Office, Fire and Aviation Management, Washington, D.C.

Flight Safety Foundation. April 1999. *Crew Error Cited As Major Cause of U.S. Aerial Fire Fighting Accidents*.

Hall, Stephen R. October 2002. The Impact of Low-Level Roles on Aircraft Structural Integrity With Particular Reference to Fire Bombers. Celeris Aerospace Canada.

HR 5102. Wildfire Response Act of 2002.

Interagency Airtanker Board Charter Revisions. Internal Briefing Paper.

Interagency Aviation Management Council. 2001. Interagency Airtanker Board Meeting Minutes. December 2, 198,1 page 1 and pages 6-8, Boise, ID; December 2-3, 1987, page 1, pages 4-6, Tucson, AZ; November 9-10, 1988 pages 1 and 4, Sacramento, CA. Internal Briefing Paper.

Interagency Aviation Management Council. January 2002. IHOG-Interagency Helicopter Operations Guide.

Interagency Call When Needed Helicopters. 2002-2004 contract. Internal Briefing Paper.

Interagency Leadplane Operations Guide. April 2002. ILOG.

Interagency Single Engine Air Tanker Operations Guide 2001/2002.

Jensen, R.S. 1996. USFS Pilot and Manager Selection. Aviation Research Associates.

Jensen, Richard. 1992. Zero-Defect Aviation in the U.S. Forest Service: Why Not? Independent Aviation Management Study. Aviation Psychology Lab, Ohio State University.

Johnson, J.P. 2001. Interagency Helicopter & Performance Index Supporting Data and White Papers. USDA Forest Service.

Langley Research Center. 1974.Operating Experiences of Retardant Bombers During Firefighting Operations. Rep. No. TM X-72622. Hampton, VA: NASA, Langley Research Center.

Larkins, William T. 1964. Forest Fire Attack System. American Aviation Historical Society Journal.

MAFFS. 2001. MAFFS/Leadplane Training.

MAFFS. 2002. Modular Airborne Fire Fighting System. Operating Plan.

Ministry of Forest, British Columbia. June 18, 1998. Request for Proposals 2000-2001 RFP Air Tanker Services.

NASA Langley Research Center. November 1974. Operating Experiences of Retardant Bombers During Firefighting Operations.

NASA. 1999. National Aerial Firefighting Safety & Efficiency Project. Ames Research Center.

National Air Tanker Service Contract RFP. Amendment 03-02. Internal Briefing Paper.

National Air Tanker Service Contract. 2002. Internal Briefing Paper.

National Transportation Safety Board. October 2001. Safety Study-Public Aircraft Safety.

NIFC Military Use Handbook. May 2002. NFES 2175.

NTSB Investigation Report. February 2002. Investigation of Loss of Beech T-34A April 1999.

NTSB Investigation Report. July 2002. Investigation of Loss of Lockheed C130A Tanker 82 August 1994.

NTSB-FAA, September 24, 2002. NTSB's Role in Public Use Aircraft Accident Investigations; FAA-Type Certification & Continued Oversight; and Flight Standards Service-Public Aircraft Operations.

Public Works and Government Services, Canada. December 2001. *Solicitation for Air Tanker Groups.*

San Dimas Technology and Development Center. 1996. Professional Helicopter Pilot Guide.

Spar Aerospace Limited. ND. Scarfo, Pierre. CC130 Aging Aircraft Initiatives.

T.O. 130 E(H)-1. ND. Operating Limits-Section V.

T.O. 1C-130A-1. ND. Operating Limits-Section V.

University of Tennessee Space Institute. 1992. *Flight Test Evaluation of the Forest Service Beechcraft B-58p Baron.* Flight Research Department.

USDA Forest Service and Department of Interior. December 1999. *Implementation Plan*

USDA Forest Service and Department of Interior. January 2000. *Management Options Team Final Report Findings and Recommendations for Tactical Aerial Resource Management Study.*

USDA Forest Service and Department of Interior. March 1995. *Phase 1, National Study of Air Tankers to Support Initial Attack and Large Fire Suppression.*

USDA Forest Service and Department of Interior. November 1996. *Phase 2, National Study of Air Tankers to Support Initial Attack and Large Fire Suppression.*

USDA Forest Service and Department of Interior. October 1998. *National Study of Tactical Aerial Resource Management to Support Initial Attack and Large Fire Suppression.*

USDA Forest Service and Department of Interior. Spring 1999. *BEAR AIR–Interagency Aviation Safety Flyer.*

USDA Forest Service Memoranda. 1992-1995. Response to *Flight Test Evaluation of the Forest Service Beechcraft B-58p Baron.* Flight Research Department, University of Tennessee Space Institute.

USDA Forest Service, April 1997. *Wildland Firefighting Helicopter Pilot Flight Evacuation Guide.*

USDA Forest Service. 1974. *National Helicopter Operations Study,* Final Report and Executive Summary.

USDA Forest Service. 1995. Aviation Management Plan. Internal Briefing Paper.

USDA Forest Service. 1995. *Infrared Operations* and *Infrared Thermal Mapping Operations Manual-NIFC.* Fire and Aviation Management.

USDA Forest Service. 2001. Aviation Safety Summary FY 2001. Internal Briefing Paper.

USDA Forest Service. August 2002. *Large Fire Review.* Rocky Mountain Region 2.

USDA Forest Service. December 1999. *Flight Operations Handbook.*

USDA Forest Service. February 2002. Aviation Program. Internal Briefing Paper.

USDA Forest Service. February 2002. Fire and Aviation Management Briefing Paper, National Fixed Wing Standardization Training Plan. Internal Briefing Paper.

USDA Forest Service. July 17, 2002. Pupulidy, Ivan. Fire and Aviation. Intermountain Region 4. Internal Briefing Paper.

USDA Forest Service. July 1989. *Aeronautical Decision Making for Natural Resource Pilots*.

USDA Forest Service. July 1993. Chief's Decision Memorandum, Airtanker Aircraft. Internal Briefing Paper.

USDA Forest Service. July 2002. Aviation Safety Summary. Internal Briefing Paper.

USDA Forest Service. March 1996. Aviation Accident and Incident Trend Study. Internal Briefing Paper.

USDA Forest Service. October 1999. *Aerial Delivered Firefighter Study*.

USDA Forest Service. October 2002. Baron Continued Airworthiness Program Southwestern Region 3. Internal Briefing Paper.

USDA Forest Service. October 2002. National Interagency Smokejumper Program. Internal Briefing Paper.

USDA Forest Service. October 2002. *Vision for Today-Vision for the Future*. Aviation Program, Pacific Southwest Region 5.

USDA Forest Service. September 2002. Aviation Strategic Plan 2003-2008. Internal Briefing Paper.

USDA Forest Service. September 2002. Aviation Training Standards. Eastern Region 9.

USDA Forest Service. September 2002. Fire and Aviation Management. Briefing Paper- Forest Service Aircraft Security. Internal Briefing Paper.

USDA Forest Service. September 2002. Inventory of Aviation Assets, Contracts, Personnel Rosters.

USDA Forest Service; USDI Bureau of Land Management; U.S. Fish and Wildlife Service. 2002. Standards for Fire and Aviation Operations 2002. Website < http://www.fire.blm.gov/Standards/2002PDF/2002Cover.pdf/>. Boise, ID: National Office of Fire and Aviation, Office of External Affairs.

USDA Office of Inspector General Audit Report. March 2002. Review of Forest Service Security Over Aircraft and Aircraft Facilities. Internal Briefing Paper.

USDI Bureau of Land Management. October 2002. Lynn, Mike. Aerial Fire Fighting-Management Considerations. Internal Briefing Paper.

Wildland Suppression Aircraft Transfer Act of 1996.